Getting Right with Lincoln

Getting Right with Lincoln

Correcting Misconceptions about Our Greatest President

Edward Steers Jr.

Foreword by Joseph Garrera

UNIVERSITY PRESS OF KENTUCKY

Scholarly publisher for the Commonwealth,
serving Bellarmine University, Berea College, Centre
College of Kentucky, Eastern Kentucky University,
The Filson Historical Society, Georgetown College,
Kentucky Historical Society, Kentucky State University,
Morehead State University, Murray State University,
Northern Kentucky University, Spalding University,
Transylvania University, University of Kentucky,
University of Louisville, and Western Kentucky University.
All rights reserved.

Editorial and Sales Offices: The University Press of Kentucky
663 South Limestone Street, Lexington, Kentucky 40508-4008
www.kentuckypress.com

Frontispiece: Photograph by Mathew B. Brady, January 8, 1864, at the Brady studio in Washington, D.C. Library of Congress.

Library of Congress Cataloging-in-Publication Data

Names: Steers, Edward, Jr., 1937– author.
Title: Getting right with Lincoln : correcting misconceptions about our
  greatest president / Edward Steers, Jr. ; foreword by Joseph Garrera.
Description: Lexington, Kentucky : The University Press of Kentucky, 2021.
  | Includes bibliographical references and index.
Identifiers: LCCN 2020046402 | ISBN 9780813180908 (hardcover) | ISBN
  9780813180915 (pdf) | ISBN 9780813180922 (epub)
Subjects: LCSH: Lincoln, Abraham, 1809–1865—Miscellanea. | Hoaxes—United
  States.
Classification: LCC E457.2 .S794 2021 | DDC 973.7092—dc23

This book is printed on acid-free paper meeting
the requirements of the American National Standard
for Permanence in Paper for Printed Library Materials.

Manufactured in the United States of America.

Member of the Association
of University Presses

To all the good people who have read my books.
I hope they provided enjoyable reading—
and some interesting history.

We learn from history that we do not learn from history.
—Georg Wilhelm Friedrich Hegel

Contents

Foreword

The study of Abraham Lincoln has inspired countless books and monographs. Despite an overwhelming amount of research and analysis, there remains contentious debate among scholars concerning major episodes in Lincoln's life.

This timely volume takes aim at a multitude of myths and incomplete evidence that animate the Lincoln story. Edward Steers Jr. was trained as a scientist, a scholar who studies facts that lead to valid conclusions based on all available evidence. Arguing with judicious skill and knowledge, Steers sets out to correct the historical record that is frequently marred by inadequate information and the lack of objective conclusions.

In nine chapters Steers rectifies some of the most prominent misconceptions about Lincoln's life. Did he have a positive relationship with his father? Was Thomas Lincoln "the poorest man that ever kept house"? Or in the larger context, was Abraham Lincoln's father a failure? These are relevant questions that help to reveal insight into Lincoln's formative and early years.

The second chapter is an exploration of a seminal question that has haunted the Lincoln canon for decades. Who wrote the famous letter to Lydia Bixby? The letter originated in November of 1864 and was sent to a grieving mother in Massachusetts who was believed to have lost five sons on the field of battle in the Civil War. Steers lays out all the evidence and explains how some past studies have taken us badly off course. What is at stake here is more than the mere authorship of the most famous letter of sympathy ever written. What is at stake is the literary brilliance of Lincoln the writer. Or does that prize go to Lincoln's masterful secretary, John Hay, the man some claim is the true author of this exceptional writing. The Bixby letter is so inspiring that it was used in the opening lines of the iconic movie *Saving Private Ryan*, when it was recited in full by Harve Presnell portraying General George Marshall.

Steers lays bare the unexpurgated historical record, applying the highest standards of research available. For example, in chapter 7, titled "The Ailing Lincoln," Steers takes aim at the popular Lincoln myth that the sixteenth president had Marfan syndrome. With the mind of a scholar and tools of a scientist, Steers explains why this theory is biased and wrong.

Throughout the book, Steers tackles myth after myth, bringing judicious research and clarity to important topics. As a scholar, Steers has been chipping away at significant Lincoln facts for four decades. With more than a dozen books to his credit, he authored *Lincoln Legends: Myths, Hoaxes and Confabulations Associated with Our Greatest President* in 2007. In the introduction to that book, Lincoln scholar Harold Holzer wrote, "Now Ed Steers, too, joins the ranks of Lincoln historians who have worked assiduously and successfully to separate fact from both fiction and folklore." Indeed, once again, as he has accomplished so many times in the past, Steers redirects our attention to seminal questions concerning Lincoln's life. Now he permanently answers nagging questions with brilliant analysis, and welcome clarity, using the full spectrum of evidence and facts.

Joseph Garrera
Lehigh Valley Heritage Museum
Allentown, Pennsylvania

Preface

Abraham Lincoln is one of those individuals whose person is so large that he has become surrounded by myth—myth that often replaces reality. It seems everyone wants to pin their tail on Abraham Lincoln's donkey. Some have espoused the theory that Lincoln was gay. Those with multiple endocrine neoplasia 2b and Marfan syndrome believe Lincoln suffered from these maladies, thereby giving greater acceptance to them. Lincoln's melancholia or depression suggests that chronic sufferers of depression might look to Lincoln to see that greatness is not immune from such sadness. It is all right to be gay, to suffer a serious cancer, or to be depressed. But Lincoln also suffered from constipation, insomnia, and occasional fits of anger. In the end, Lincoln could be all things to all people.

To those attracted by the lure of revisionism, Lincoln was a racist. Even those who believe in Lincoln's greatness believe he preferred colonization to citizenship for blacks. To others, he was a "stone-cold racist." He moved too slowly on emancipation, hated his father, and his marriage was made in hell. Had Lincoln not been assassinated, he would have died in office from his life-threatening diseases.

It is a fact that Lincoln scholars are divided in their written descriptions of Lincoln as a child, a young man, and a president. They sometimes quarrel over his relationship with his father, his wife, and even his alleged lover. They differ over his assassination: he was killed under orders from the pope, his own secretary of war, Jefferson Davis—or all three.

Sources are the determining factor in biographical history. Historians rely on primary documents, letters, diaries, recorded speeches, and firsthand accounts. Secondarily, they rely on the testimony and reminiscences of people who have some connection with their subject. Often, these connections are close, while in other instances they are separated by many years, relying on memory, or on secondary sources, what the law refers to as hearsay. The further one gets from the subject, in both time and place, the less reliable the testimony becomes. And yet, in many instances it is our only source of information.

In Lincoln's case we have a collection of documents covering much of his life known as *The Collected Works of Abraham Lincoln*, edited by Lincoln historian Roy P. Basler. We can rely on this collection in assessing Lincoln since it is generated by Lincoln. Second, we have several primary documents accumulated in courthouses that deal with the everyday life of the Lincoln family that have been published in secondary sources. Third, we have an excellent study titled *Recollected Words of Abraham Lincoln*, edited and evaluated as to both accuracy and reliability by two respected historians, Don E. Fehrenbacher and his wife, Virginia Fehrenbacher. Fourth, and perhaps most heavily relied on for understanding the intimate aspects of Lincoln, are the reminiscences of individuals who bear a range of relationships to the subject, from intimate to casual. This latter source is the work of Douglas L. Wilson and Rodney O. Davis, known as *Herndon's Informants*. This work, however, is fraught with danger, and historians need to tread carefully when relying on it for source material. As Lincoln scholar James G. Randall reminds us, it is a collection of reminiscences based on "dim and misty" memory.

Individuals rely on memory, and their relationship to the subject, often decades after the fact, which can be seriously flawed. There is the temptation to embellish and to make one seem more important than is truthful. And last, we have the propensity of historians to want to tell an interesting story. Too often, many biographers wind up making a whole shirt out of a few buttons. This is understandable because historians are, after all, storytellers. Lincoln receives a telegram while visiting the War Department telegraph office. It tells of the death of a close friend. Lincoln's eyes fill with tears as he rises and makes his way from the building clutching the telegram in his hand. He is so distraught at the news that he stumbles along the path leading to the White House, where he walks past a line of visitors, waving them away. "I am too deeply grieved to see anyone just now," he says as he slowly climbs the stairs to his office. It is a good story for which there is no reliable evidence. Still, it does fit Lincoln's character rather closely, and is behavior we can readily believe. We all know that wonderfully pleasant-sounding lyric attributed to Lincoln, "You can fool some of the people all of the time, and all of the people some of the time, but you can't fool all of the people all of the time." Only it appears that it was P. T. Barnum who coined the phrase, not Abraham Lincoln. As in most such cases, it is not Lincoln who made such claims, but rather his admirers who are to blame—and who can blame them, for if Lincoln did not say it, he easily could have.

Getting Right with Lincoln is a reaction on the part of the author to what is seen as the wrong side of revisionist history. It is that attractive revisionist lure that some authors appear unable to resist. Lincoln may have hated his father, his marriage, been a hidden racist, and suffered from lethal diseases, but there is no solid evidence to support such claims. In fact, in every instance the evidence refutes such claims, and yet they persist. This book is an attempt to provide the other side of the coin, and get right with Lincoln.

The young Lincoln as portrayed in an exhibit in the Abraham Lincoln Presidential Library and Museum in Springfield, Illinois. Photograph by Edward Steers Jr.

The Shiftless Father Myth

Like with so much of the Lincoln story, historians are divided on most events from his pre-presidential years. Many of Lincoln's biographers write sparingly of his years as a youth growing up in Kentucky and Indiana, leaving the reader with the impression they are unimportant to the overall story of Lincoln. Justifiably, Lincoln's presidency is the epic story of his life, but to understand Lincoln the president it is essential to understand his formative years, including his environment. It is here where many historians fall short.

Psychologists tell us that a child's brain develops more during the first few years of life than at any other time. The brain's growth during this early period is more rapid. Sixty percent of a baby's energy goes into brain development. The remaining 40 percent must do for all the other vital organs combined, which shows just how important the brain is to a developing organism. By the third year, a healthy brain will have formed one thousand trillion *connections*, a number beyond comprehension![1] It is in the temporal lobes, which regulate emotions, and a person's senses, that early childhood conditions are critical. PET scans (Positron Emission Tomography) have shown that deprivation in infancy results in severe emotional and cognitive problems.[2]

Nature and nurture are critical to human development. While nurture (environment) influences a child's development, to be sure, genetics (nature) plays the dominant role. In most cases, genetics can override the effects of nurture, both positive and negative. While genetics may be dominant in determining character, nurture is the essential ingredient for development. What do we know of Lincoln's early years, and of the father and mother who made the man who became our greatest president?

The historical record of Abraham Lincoln's formative years has been like a metronome, swinging back and forth between a sometimes cruel, poverty-stricken childhood and one filled "with mirth and glee,"[3] a young boyhood of youthful adventure and learning. In some interpretations, the youthful Lincoln is described as "misery's child," who was subjected to "cruelty and degeneracy" by his father,[4] while others say he had "a joyous, happy boyhood" and a home conducive to good morals.[5] Cruel and degenerate, or joyous and happy? I suppose it is possible Lincoln experienced both, but with only dim and misty memories to rely on, what are we to believe? Is there a primary record we can turn to? Are there surviving examples to judge?

Born on the twelfth of February 1809, Lincoln had very little to say about his youth. In fact, Lincoln had little to say about much of his life. His law partner of twenty-one years, and close friend and early biographer, William Herndon, described Lincoln as "the most shut-mouthed man" he ever knew, and yet volumes have been written on Lincoln's musings, beliefs, and private thoughts in general. Much of these writings are drawn from the recollections of people who knew Lincoln—some intimately, some casually, and most recorded years after he died.

It is interesting to see that the joyous boyhood of Lincoln can be ascribed to his two mothers, his birth mother, Nancy Hanks Lincoln, and Sarah Bush Johnston Lincoln, his stepmother, while the cruel and degenerate boyhood of Lincoln falls on the shoulders of the allegedly miscreant father, Thomas Lincoln. We are treated to this dichotomy and left to choose which life (and which parent) we prefer.

The Lincoln story shows this dichotomy. Lincoln allegedly told Herndon, "All that I am or hope to be I get from my mother, God bless her," and follows the statement by saying that his mother "was the illegitimate daughter of a nobleman." Lincoln then went on to say, "Did you never notice that bastards are generally smarter, shrewder, and more intellectual than others?" attributing his gifted qualities to both nurture (mother) and nature (genetics).[6] Lincoln apparently felt that he inherited his intellectual qualities from the "nobleman" who took advantage of his grandmother, Lucy Hanks, passing his superior genes on to Lincoln by way of his mother (not his father).

While Lincoln's birth mother and stepmother survive the acid pens of historians, his father does not. Few people have suffered more at the hands of historians than Thomas Lincoln. And this negative view was calculated from early on, shortly after Lincoln became president. The generally accepted characterization of Thomas Lincoln is that of a failure. Often perceived as lazy, slothful, and financially inept, his worst quality in the eyes of these historians is that of being a bad, even indifferent father. Such views are often constructed by cherry-picking the evidence and applying a selective view that discards the flesh and keeps the pits.

Michael Burlingame champions many of the negative descriptions of Thomas Lincoln and his treatment of his young son, Abraham. In his impressive two-volume biography of Lincoln, *Abraham Lincoln: A Life*, and in his earlier book, *The Inner Life of Abraham Lincoln*, Burlingame launches a revisionist assault across the broad spectrum of Lincoln's relationship with his father. Countering Burlingame's view is the more positive view of Thomas Lincoln that comes from Louis A. Warren. Warren's writings on the subject are often referred to as the "Warren school," while the negative view is represented by what may be called the "Burlingame school."

It is in the relationship between Thomas Lincoln and his son, Abraham, that historians focus their most severe criticism. In recent years, the Burlingame school appears to have won the battle. Like most everything associated with Abraham Lincoln, there is

Traditional portrait of Thomas
Lincoln, photographer unknown.
Library of Congress.

ample material on both sides of the ledger. The traditionalists support a rather positive view of Thomas Lincoln, while the revisionists support a more negative view of him.

Current historians too often ignore Louis A. Warren, who was the first to undertake a considerable amount of research into the early courthouse records in Kentucky. His book on Lincoln's parentage and childhood is absent from most modern Lincoln bibliographies.[7] Likewise, William E. Barton's two books on Lincoln's paternity and on his lineage are also absent.[8] This may well be due to their findings having been published in the first quarter of the twentieth century. This is unfortunate because, while the research of these two scholars appeared a century ago, their findings have stood the test of time and should form the basis for any study on the Lincolns of Kentucky and Indiana. Warren published much of his findings in a little-known but extensive archive known as *The Lincoln Kinsman,* a series of fifty-two pamphlets covering decades of research in virtu-

Artist conception of Nancy Hanks Lincoln by Lloyd Ostendorf. Original art by Lloyd Ostendorf, used with permission.

ally every aspect of the Lincoln and Hanks families. Much of Warren's findings, mostly from courthouse records, cannot be found published in standard sources, and they are an essential resource for writing of Lincoln's early life.[9]

Burlingame writes that Lincoln was ashamed of his family background and the poverty he experienced as a child.[10] William Herndon would agree. He wrote, "Lincoln rose from a lower depth than any of them—from a stagnant, putrid pool."[11] One gets the sense that the more depraved Lincoln's childhood, the greater his success in overcoming the "putrid pool" and rising to the presidency. In fact, such a contrast is exactly what many historians point to in their praise of Lincoln.

Not all historians agree with this dismal view of Lincoln's youth or the slothful father. Louis A. Warren, who championed both Thomas Lincoln and Nancy Hanks Lincoln, wrote, "Thomas Lincoln has been the scapegoat for all who would make Lincoln a saint . . .

folklore and tradition have made him one of the most despised characters in American history."[12] To Warren's detractors, Abraham Lincoln was a man who was born not with a silver spoon in his mouth, but one made from a thorny branch of the locust tree.

It is true that Lincoln told his early biographer, John Locke Scripps, "It is a great piece of folly to attempt to make anything out of my early life. It can all be condensed into a single sentence, and that sentence you will find in Gray's Elegy; the short and simple annals of the poor."[13] But this is a far cry from "a stagnant, putrid pool" and an abusive father. There is nothing in Lincoln's recorded or recollected words that suggest he came from such a lowly place. The hardscrabble life experienced by most families on the American frontier was commonplace. The Lincolns were no exception.

One former neighbor said that Thomas Lincoln was "the poorest man that ever kept house."[14] This conclusion simply does not concur with the known facts. Thomas Lincoln was solvent for most of his life, and there was never a time when he did not own property or pay his bills. What we know about Thomas Lincoln's financial dealings comes primarily from the research of Louis A. Warren and William E. Barton, two early-twentieth-century historians who have disappeared from modern Lincoln biographies. This is a shame, for these two early scholars uncovered a significant number of primary documents in courthouse records that tell us a great deal about Thomas Lincoln's financial dealings and community life. They present facts, not conjecture.

It turns out that Thomas owned eight properties for which he paid cash. He appears on several tax rolls (never delinquent), owned several horses and livestock, successfully bid in at least two auctions (paying cash), and left behind a dozen examples of highly skilled cabinetwork that can be found on display in museums and historical societies.

Thomas Lincoln's early years are marked by success. On the

death of his father, Abraham Lincoln, at the hands of Indians by ambush in 1786, Thomas, just eight years old, moved with his widowed mother, Bersheba (Bathsheba), and two older brothers, Mordecai and Josiah, and sisters Mary and Nancy, to the Beech Fork community in Washington County, Kentucky, approximately fifty miles east of their home on Long Run near Louisville. We believe she did this to be near her husband's wealthy cousin, Hannaniah Lincoln, whom she could rely on for protection, both physical and financial.

Although Abraham Lincoln, Thomas Lincoln's father, died in 1786, a record of his estate does not appear until ten years later, in 1796. In that tabulation the following property is listed: 100 acres on Beech Fork, 400 acres on Floyd's Fork (also known as "Long Run"), two tracts of 1,000 acres each on the Kentucky River, and two tracts on the Green River of 800 acres and 1,134 acres, respectively. In all, the father of Thomas Lincoln appears to have owned just over 5,500 acres of Kentucky land at the time of his death, hardly an example of poverty.[15]

The rule of primogeniture, commonly practiced at the time, saw the estate of Thomas's father pass to the eldest son, Mordecai. While Mordecai inherited the land and assets of his father, it appears he shared a part of the inheritance with his two younger brothers, Thomas and Josiah. Lincoln historian William E. Barton concluded that Mordecai shared a part of the proceeds from his father's estate with his two younger brothers because both brothers paid cash to purchase farms shortly after the estate was settled.[16] In 1797, Josiah bought a farm in the Beech Fork area, and in 1803 Thomas, now twenty-five years old, purchased the Mill Creek farm near Elizabethtown. It was just before the purchase of these two farms that Mordecai sold off several of his father's holdings. Barton concludes that Mordecai was the source of the money for the purchases since neither Josiah nor Thomas had any income to speak of to pay cash for the two properties.[17]

The Elizabethtown cabin. From a postcard, circa 1940. Edward Steers Jr. collection.

Thomas Lincoln lived thirty-six of his first forty-four years in Kentucky, from 1780 to 1816. During that period he owned three farms and two lots in Elizabethtown. On one of the lots he built a house for his new bride, Nancy Hanks. He was regularly listed on the tax rolls in both Washington County (Beech Fork) and Hardin County (Mill Creek), and records show that he paid his taxes on a timely basis in cash. During this period he owned from one to three horses and various livestock, including cows and oxen. He attended at least two auctions, purchased several items, and paid cash in each instance. In 1795 he served in the Washington County militia for a period of thirty days, from June through July, and in 1805 he served in Hardin County's 3rd Regiment of militia and was elected "Ensign" (second lieutenant) by his fellow militiamen, certainly a mark of respect.[18]

Between the years 1803 and 1806, Thomas Lincoln served as a constable, which required him to post a bond. He also served on at least two juries and on a road-building committee. In 1814, while living at the Knob Creek property, Thomas was chosen by the court as an appraiser of a neighbor's estate.[19] While none of this speaks to the relationship with his son, it does support a positive view of his financial status and his character, as well as his elevated status within the community.

In 1803, Thomas Lincoln purchased his first farm in Hardin County, Kentucky. He paid 118 pounds for the 238 acres on Mill Creek.[20] Three years later, in 1806, he returned to the Beech Fork community, where he married Nancy Hanks on June 10, 1806, in the home of her guardian, Richard Berry. The tax year for 1807 shows that Thomas purchased a lot in Elizabethtown on which he built a cabin for his new bride while retaining ownership of the Mill Creek farm. He purchased several kitchen items, including a dish, several spoons, a basin, and even a sword, paying $8.92 cash for the lot.[21] It was in the Elizabethtown home that Thomas and Nancy's first child, Sarah, was born.

The following year, Thomas moved his family to a new farm near Nolan Creek known as "The Sinking Spring Farm." This farm is now a national historic site administered by the National Park Service and contains the traditional Lincoln birth cabin. For this farm, Thomas Lincoln paid $200 in cash.[22] By the time his son, Abraham, was born on February 12, Thomas Lincoln owned the Mill Creek farm, two lots in Elizabethtown (valued at $40 for tax purposes), and the Sinking Spring farm. These properties represent a substantial holding for a thirty-one-year-old man with a wife and two children. In 1814, he was listed fifteenth out of eighty-nine property owners for tax purposes, placing him in the top fifth of property owners in the county.[23]

The homes appear to be standard for the period. From a modern perspective we frequently equate log homes with poor circumstances, which is simply not the case. There are numerous records of Thomas Lincoln purchasing household goods, livestock, and farm implements, indicating a reasonably well-stocked home and farm. He

The traditional birthplace cabin. Library of Congress.

even purchased a toy wagon at auction for his young son.[24] These are hardly the actions of a slothful, harsh father who mistreated his child.

Thomas Lincoln lost both of his Kentucky farms not because he failed to pay for them, which he did, but because of Kentucky's faulty land titles and inaccurate land surveys. Thomas Lincoln bought the two farms not knowing the sellers did not hold proper titles. He was not the only victim. The loss of farms throughout the region hit most of the landowners. Giving up his Knob Creek farm in 1816 and moving to Indiana, Thomas filed suit to recover his money as the innocent victim of a faulty title. He eventually won the suit, and the court ordered that he should recover his full purchase price, but having moved to Indiana, he never returned to Kentucky to collect his money.[25]

For the better part of his life Thomas Lincoln was financially solvent and a respected member of the communities in which he lived. A full accounting of his financial transactions can be found in

Louis Warren's article in *The Lincoln Kinsman*.[26] Lincoln scholar Michael Burlingame devotes a fair amount of verbiage to describing Lincoln's father in disparaging terms in his two-volume biography of Abraham Lincoln.[27] He begins by focusing on Thomas Lincoln's carpentry skills, describing them as "so rudimentary that people called him a 'rough' and 'cheap carpenter' who could only 'put doors, windows, and floors in log houses' and do a tolerable job of joining."[28] As an example, Burlingame writes, "In 1807, Denton Geoghegan of Elizabethtown refused to pay Thomas for hewing timbers for his sawmill. Geoghegan claimed some timbers were too short, others too long."[29] Geoghegan refused to pay Thomas Lincoln, and Lincoln filed suit against Geoghegan in Magistrate's Court on March 25, 1807. He won his claim. The court dismissed the case, and Geoghegan was ordered to pay Lincoln and the court costs. On review, it was decided that Lincoln fulfilled the contract in a "workman-like manner."[30]

When it comes to Thomas Lincoln's carpentry skills, Burlingame's assessment appears to miss the mark by quite a bit. There are at least twelve surviving examples of Thomas Lincoln's skill as a cabinetmaker, ten of which are on display in various museums. These pieces, several examined by the author, are well made and show a high level of craftsmanship, well beyond "rough" and "cheap." The most elegant is a cherry wood "fall front desk," which Thomas Lincoln made for Dr. Crook of Spencer County, Indiana. The desk now resides in the Abraham Lincoln Presidential Library and Museum in Springfield, Illinois. Among the other pieces are a walnut mantel (in the officers' club at Fort Knox, Kentucky), five corner cabinets, and a day bed. Thomas Lincoln's skill as a first-rate cabinetmaker is obvious from these surviving examples.

Perhaps the most telling description of Thomas Lincoln as a cabinetmaker comes from his nearest neighbor in Indiana, near the town of Gentryville, John Romine. In an interview with William Herndon in September 1865, Romine told Herndon, "Thomas Lin-

Dr. Crook's cherry desk, circa 1825. Taper Collection, Abraham Lincoln Presidential Library and Museum.

Corner cupboard, circa 1814. Abraham Lincoln Library and Museum at Lincoln Memorial University.

Mantel from the Hardin Thomas house, now in the officers' club at Fort Knox, Kentucky. Photograph by Edward
Steers Jr.

coln was a carpenter by trade—relied on it for a living—*not on farming*" (emphasis added).[31]

It is true that late in life Thomas Lincoln began to experience
financial problems and turned to his now successful son for help.
But this was at a time in his sixties when his health was failing after
his move to Goosenest Prairie, Illinois, in 1834. By age sixty he had
lost the sight of one eye and the second was deteriorating, leaving
Thomas Lincoln nearly blind. He died in 1851 at the age of seventy-three, in all likelihood from the effects of type 2 diabetes.

While much of what we know about Thomas Lincoln's financial
life comes from Warren and Barton, much of what we know about
Thomas Lincoln's personal life comes from the research of William
Herndon. Herndon interviewed several neighbors and associates of
Lincoln from his early years in Kentucky, Indiana, and New Salem in

Dennis Friend Hanks. Library of Congress.

preparation for writing his own biography of Lincoln. These interviews and letters are published in a single volume edited by Douglas L. Wilson and Rodney O. Davis.[32]

The chief witness concerning Thomas and Abraham Lincoln's early life for most researchers, including Herndon, is Dennis Hanks. Hanks was ten years Lincoln's senior and lived with the Lincoln family in Indiana from 1818 to 1821 following the deaths of his adoptive parents. Dennis was the illegitimate son of Lincoln's great aunt, Nancy Hanks (who was Nancy Hanks Lincoln's aunt and sister to Lucy Hanks), and Charles Friend. He was raised in the household of his aunt and uncle, Elizabeth and Thomas Sparrow. The Sparrows died from "milk sickness" in 1818, near the same time that Abraham Lincoln's mother died from the same disease (see chapter 6).

Dennis was nineteen years old when he moved into the household of Thomas Lincoln; Abraham was nine. Dennis followed Thomas Lincoln when he moved to Illinois in 1830 and spent his later years
living with the extended family of Thomas Lincoln at Goosenest
Prairie. He was killed when run down by a carriage in 1892 while returning from a celebration commemorating the passage of the Thirteenth Amendment.[33]

While Dennis Hanks's close association with the Lincoln family makes him the best source of information on the Lincolns during
these early years, it does not always make him the most reliable. The
complications biographers face include Dennis's unreliability in certain specifics of his testimony. Known to embellish his role as a biographer of the Lincoln family and a close friend of Abraham Lincoln,
Dennis's statements have to be analyzed as anecdotes and, where
possible, corroborated. An example is his attempt to legitimize the
birth of Lincoln's mother, Nancy Hanks.

The effort to disparage Lincoln by pointing out that his mother
was a bastard was prevalent among his enemies, especially throughout the Southern states during his presidency, and after his death by
many neo-Confederates. By the same token, some biographers attempted to show how special Lincoln became by contrasting his alleged poverty and "white trash" parents with his rising above them
to the presidency.

We now know from mitochondrial DNA analysis (mtDNA) that
Nancy Hanks was the daughter of Lucy Hanks, as historians believed.[34] Dennis, in an apparent attempt to legitimize Lincoln's
mother, consistently lied about her birth, claiming she was the legitimate daughter of Henry Sparrow and Lucy Hanks Sparrow. Lucy
lived with Henry Sparrow for several years as his common law wife
before marrying him. Yet, Nancy Hanks, Lincoln's mother, was born
years before Lucy moved in with Henry Sparrow.

In an interview with William Herndon, Dennis Hanks stated:

"Thos at the age of 25 was married to Nancy Sparrow—not Hanks as stated in the Biographies of the day—Nancy Sparrow—Abraham's mother was the child of Henry Sparrow. Henry Sparrow's wife was Lucy Hanks—Abraham's grandmother. The stories going about, charging wrong or indecency prostitution in any of the above families is false—and got up by base political enemies & trattors to injure A. Lincolns reputation—name and fame."[35] Dennis clearly lied about Lincoln's mother being the legitimate daughter of Lucy Hanks Sparrow and Henry Sparrow.

As to Dennis's reminiscences of his cousin Abraham, he wrote in a letter to Herndon in June 1865, "You ask Did Thos Lincoln trate Abe cruly. He loved him. I never could tell whether Abe Loved his farther Very well or not. I don't think he did for Abe was one of those forward boys. I have seen his father Nock him down of the fence when a stranger would Call for information to a neighbours house. Abe always would have the first word."[36] On more than one occasion, Thomas Lincoln apparently disciplined his son for "rudeness" for speaking to adults first rather than waiting for his father to speak.

Conversely, seven months later Dennis Hanks wrote in a letter to William Herndon that "Mr. Thomas Lincoln was a good, clean, social, truthful & honest man, loving like his wife Evry thing & every body . . . the Old Man Loved his children."[37] Later in the same letter he said, "Abe was a good boy—an affectionate one—a boy who loved his father & mother dearly."[38] Clearly, these statements contradict one another.

Sarah Bush Johnston Lincoln, Thomas's second wife and Abraham Lincoln's stepmother, gave an extensive interview to Herndon in September 1865. In it she spoke of her husband and stepson, "When Abe was reading My husband took particular Care not to disturb him. . . . Mr. Lincoln never made Abe quit reading to do anything if he could avoid it. He would do it himself first . . . he wanted, as he himself felt the uses & necessities of Education his boy Abraham to learn & he Encouraged him to do it in all ways he could."[39]

Traditional photograph of Sarah Bush Johnston Lincoln. Photographer unknown. National Park Service.

Sarah Bush Johnston Lincoln was the closest person to Abraham Lincoln throughout his growing years. She was always present in his early life. In an interview by Herndon she said, "Abe never gave me a cross word or look and never refused in fact, or Even in appearance, to do any thing I requested him. His mind & mine—what little I had seemed to run together—to move in the same channel."[40]

Of course, Sarah Lincoln's testimony about her husband and his treatment of his son has to be seen through the prism of her relationship to both. One assumes she would be reluctant to say anything that might reflect poorly on her deceased husband. By the same token, she was a woman who was described as a bright and honest person who spoke forthrightly. Rather than lie, she would, in all likelihood, avoid answering Herndon's questions. But it should be noted that Thomas had been dead for fourteen years when she wrote to Herndon.

Dennis Hanks, on the other hand, constantly describes himself as playing an important role in the young Lincoln's life. In his interview with Herndon, Dennis is quick to point out that he was the one who "taught Abe his first lesson in spelling—reading & writing—I taught Abe to write with a buzzards quill—put Abe's hand in mine & moving his fingers by my hand to give him the idea how to write."[41] This appears to be another exaggeration of Dennis's, as Lincoln apparently was taught to read and write by his mother, Nancy Lincoln, skills that were furthered by his attending school for six months while living at Knob Creek.[42]

Contrasting this image of Lincoln and his father are the comments from Michael Burlingame's two-volume history. Burlingame points out that Thomas Lincoln "rented his boy" and forced him to hand over his meager earnings. "Lincoln," Burlingame writes, "was virtually a slave . . . locked in bondage" feeling "as if he were a chattel on a Southern plantation declaring in later life, 'I used to be a slave.'"[43] These quotations are from a newspaper article written by John E. Roll, a friend from Lincoln's New Salem past. The actual quote reads: "I remember one time in a speech he made at the courthouse, that time he said the country could not live half slave and half free, he said *we were all slaves one time or another* [emphasis added], but that white men could make themselves free and the negroes could not. He said: 'There is my old friend John Roll. He used to be a slave, but he made himself free, and I used to be a slave, and now I am so free that they let me practice law.' I remember that." Lincoln's reference to being a slave seems more jocular than literal.[44] The actual quote cannot be found in the two primary sources used by most scholars: *Herndon's Informants* and *Recollected Words of Abraham Lincoln*.

The political savant Sidney Blumenthal is the latest critic of the relationship between Thomas Lincoln and his son. He quotes Thomas Lincoln as remarking to a friend, "I suppose that Abe is still fooling hisself with eddication. I tried to stop it, but he has got that fool idea in his head, and it can't be got out."[45] Unfortunately, Blumenthal gives no reference to support this rather precise and damaging quotation. Thomas, Blumenthal writes, took Abe's cleverness as pointed humiliation, as his son somehow trying to show him up by "acting smart." So much of Blumenthal's early description of Thomas Lincoln lacks any factual basis or sourcing, and is simply wrong. Blumenthal claims Thomas Lincoln was "abandoned by his stepmother" (I presume he means Bersheba Herring Lincoln), married the daughter of "Lucy Shipley," and served on a "local slave patrol to catch runaways."[46]

Thomas lived with his mother and siblings in the Beech Fork community from 1786 until he moved to his Mill Creek farm in 1803.[47] She never abandoned him, nor did he abandon her. He moved her, and his sister and brother-in-law, to the Mill Creek area when he married Nancy Hanks in 1806.[48] Mitochondrial DNA analysis has proven that Nancy Hanks bears no genetic relationship to the Shipley family,[49] and Thomas Lincoln was known to oppose slavery. He moved to Indiana in part because of Kentucky's slave policies.[50] It is true that he served as sheriff for a period of time, but there is no record that his service involved a "slave patrol." Without citations it is impossible to verify any of Blumenthal's claims.

The most damning case Michael Burlingame makes in support of his claim that Lincoln was estranged from his father comes late in both the father's and son's lives. In 1851, Thomas Lincoln, age seventy-three, was grievously ill and dying. Lincoln received a letter from his stepbrother, John D. Johnston, notifying him of his father's condition, and that he was not expected to recover. Lincoln responds in a letter to his stepbrother explaining why he cannot visit his dying father:

> You already know I desire that neither Father or Mother shall
> be in want of any comfort either in health or sickness while
> they live; and I feel sure you have not failed to use my name, if

necessary, to procure a doctor, or anything else for Father in his present sickness. My business is such that I could hardly leave home now, if it were not, as it is, that my own wife is sick-abed. (It is a case of baby-sickness, and I suppose not danger-ous.)[51] I sincerely hope that Father may yet recover his health; but at all events tell him to remember to call upon, and confide in, our great, and good, and merciful Maker; who will not turn away from him in any extremity. He notes the fall of a sparrow, and numbers the hairs of our heads; and He will not forget the dying man, who puts his trust in Him. Say to him that if we could meet now, it is doubtful whether it would not be more painful than pleasant; but that if it be his lot to go now, he will soon have a joyous meeting with many loved ones gone before; and where the rest of us, through the help of God, hope ere-long to join them.[52]

In the eyes of Thomas Lincoln's detractors, Lincoln's statement that it would "be more painful than pleasant" shows Lincoln's dislike or low regard for his father. Burlingame refers to this passage as "cold." He further writes, "Lincoln neither attended Thomas's funeral nor arranged for a tombstone to mark his grave."[53] One assumes it is the reference to their meeting as being "painful" that shows Lincoln's dislike for his father. The question is whether Lincoln in using the word "painful" meant sorrow or instead meant dislike, as Burlingame suggests.

Attorney and Lincoln scholar Richard E. Hart, past president of the Abraham Lincoln Association, took on this very question in an article in that association's newsletter. "What son would write such a cruel letter to his 73-year-old father in his final moments of life?" Hart points out that it would be Lincoln's beloved stepmother that would feel the sting of such a mean-spirited comment—the step-mother Lincoln dearly loved.

That Lincoln did not attend his father's funeral is further evidence of Lincoln's disdain for his father, we are told. But, as Hart points out, it again would be Sarah Lincoln that would be injured by such a slight, not Thomas, who was dead. Hart rightly concludes that

Shiloh Church Cemetery. Photograph by Edward Steers Jr.

Lincoln did not attend his father's funeral because of his wife's "baby-sickness" from the birth of Willie Lincoln, and the recent death of Eddy that still lay heavy over Mary Lincoln.[54] It should be noted that Mary and Abraham did not attend the funeral of Mary's father, Robert Todd, in 1849 in Lexington, Kentucky, and that Lincoln did not arrange for a tombstone for his own mother, Nancy Hanks Lincoln, whom he dearly loved. If the absence of providing a tombstone for his father shows Lincoln's disdain, then it also shows his disdain for his mother, which we know is untrue. And, let us not forget that Abraham Lincoln named his fourth son Thomas, after his recently deceased father.[55]

In an effort to support my comments favoring Thomas Lincoln in his relationship with his son, I have tended to cherry-pick the evidence to cast the father in a positive light. But by the same token, so do Thomas Lincoln's detractors in an effort to cast him in a negative light. The difference is in providing reliable sources and appropriate citations. This is the very problem in studying the life of Abraham

Original tombstone of
Thomas Lincoln damaged
by souvenir hunters.
Photograph by Edward
Steers Jr.

Modern tombstone of
Thomas and Sarah Lincoln.
Photograph by Edward
Steers Jr.

Lincoln. More than with most figures in American history, there are frequently two sides to every aspect of Abraham Lincoln's life (and death), whether it is the alleged love affair with Ann Rutledge, his position on colonization and slavery, his abuse of presidential powers, or who was behind his death. Eminent historians fall on both sides of most issues involving Lincoln. The good, or the bad, too often reflect the subjective views of the biographer. While we all have the same facts available to us, we often draw different conclusions.

Lincoln best expressed the problem in a story he allegedly told about a court case where he was the defense lawyer: "A farmer was working in his barnyard one day when his ten-year-old son came rushing up to him, all excited. 'Paw,' the boy said. 'Come quick. The hired hand and Sis are up in the haymow, and he's a pullin' down his pants and she's aliftin' up her skirts. Paw, they're gettin' ready to pee all over our hay.' 'Son,' said the farmer, 'you've got your facts right, it's your conclusions that are wrong.'"[56]

While we historians may get our facts right, too often it is our conclusions that are wrong.

Only known image of Lydia Bixby. Photographer unknown. Wikimedia Commons.

A Case of Identity Theft
Abraham Lincoln, John Hay, and the Widow Bixby

In an article in the winter 1995 issue of the *Journal of the Abraham Lincoln Association,* Lincoln historian Michael Burlingame published the first of two articles claiming Abraham Lincoln was not the author of the famous letter to the widow Lydia Bixby attributed to him. It was not a new claim. Burlingame bolstered his argument by quoting journalist David Rankin Barbee: "The furious controversies that have raged [around the Bixby letter's authorship] threatened to become as important in the annals of this country as *le affair Dreyfus* was in France, with this difference—no scandal, though a lot of dirt and deception, attaches to it; no duels, except verbal ones, have been fought over it; and no one . . . has been imprisoned because of it."[1] It was an old claim. Nicholas Murray Butler, president of Columbia University from 1902 until 1940, in his autobiography, claimed that John Morley, the eminent British biographer of William Gladstone, claimed that Lincoln's secretary John Hay told him he had written the Bixby letter, but not to tell anyone until after Hay's death. Morley did so, only telling Butler after Hay died. Morley asked Butler not to tell anyone until after he, Morley, died. It appears Hay did not follow his own edict, telling two friends, W. C. Brownell and Walter Hines Page, that he was the author of the letter, once again swearing the two men to not reveal the secret until he died.[2] Thus, we have several instances of hearsay.

Lydia Bixby was a middle-aged widow who, having been born in Virginia, subsequently wound up living in Boston, Massachusetts.

She was the mother of five sons who served in the Union army who she claimed were killed in battle. Having moved seven times within a period of two years, there is reason to believe she operated a brothel at one point during her Boston years.[3] She was catapulted into fame by the now famous letter sent to her by Abraham Lincoln, a heartfelt letter meant to provide a small measure of consolation for a mother's terrible loss.

> Executive Mansion Washington, Nov. 21, 1864
> To Mrs Bixby, Boston, Mass.
> Dear Madam.
>
> I have been shown in the files of the War Department a statement of the Adjutant General of Massachusetts that you are the mother of five sons who have died gloriously on the field of battle. I feel how weak and fruitless must be any word of mine which should attempt to beguile you from the grief of a loss so overwhelming. But I cannot refrain from tendering to you the consolation that may be found in the thanks of the republic they died to save. I pray that our Heavenly Father may assuage the anguish of your bereavement, and leave you only the cherished memory of the loved and lost, and the solemn pride that must be yours to have laid so costly a sacrifice upon the altar of freedom.
>
> Yours very sincerely and respectfully,
>
> A. Lincoln.[4]

Mrs. Bixby's claim that her five sons were killed in battle was supported by the adjutant general of Massachusetts, William Schouler. Mrs. Bixby, it seems, was the basis for the belief her five sons were all killed. She visited the office of Schouler and showed him five letters from each of her five sons' commanding officers informing her of the death of her sons.

Accepting Mrs. Bixby's claim at face value, Schouler wrote to the governor of Massachusetts, John Andrew, informing him of the

Pathetic Letter of the President to a Poor Widow.

BOSTON, Nov. 25.—Mrs. Bixby, the recipient of the following letter from President Lincoln, is a poor widow living in the Eleventh ward of this city. Her sixth son, who was severely wounded in a recent battle, is now lying in the Readville hospital:

"EXECUTIVE MANSION, }
"WASHINGTON, Nov. 21, 1864. }

"DEAR MADAM: I have been shown on the file of the War Department a statement of the Adjutant General of Massachusetts, that you are the mother of five sons who have died gloriously on the field of battle.

"I feel how weak and fruitless must be any word of mine which should attempt to beguile you from the grief of a loss so overwhelming; but I cannot refrain from tendering to you the consolation that may be found in the thanks of the republic they died to save.

"I pray that our Heavenly Father may assuage the anguish of your bereavements, and leave only the cherished memory of the loved and lost, and the solemn pride that must be yours, to have laid so costly a sacrifice upon the altar of freedom.

"Yours, very sincerely and respectfully,
"A. LINCOLN.
"To Mrs. BIXBY, Boston, Mass."

Clipping of the Bixby letter from the *Boston Transcript*, November 25, 1864. Edward Steers Jr. collection.

woman's tragic loss and adding a personal note, "Mrs. Bixby is the best specimen of a true-hearted Union woman I have yet seen."[5] Andrew was deeply moved by Mrs. Bixby's case and sent a letter to the adjutant general of the United States, writing, "This is a case so remarkable, that I really wish a letter might be written her by the President of the United States, taking notice of a noble mother of five dead heroes so well deserved."[6] The adjutant general responded to Andrew's request by asking for the names, regiments, and companies of the five sons. Also requested were the dates of each son's death, and the battles in which they were killed. This request was forwarded to Mrs. Bixby, relying on her to provide the important information.

That Lincoln sent the letter is a fact. Copies were released to the Boston newspapers, and the text of the letter appeared the following day. The Democratic-controlled newspapers panned the letter as pitiful and a cheap political ploy on the part of the president, while the Republican-controlled newspapers praised the president for his empathy and moving words to a distraught widow. Lydia Bixby was hardly distraught. Much of the evidence that has come to light over the years suggests she was something of a con artist and cheat. Although two of her sons were indeed killed, the other three survived. One was honorably discharged following his capture and subsequent parole (released to the custody of the Union army), the second deserted to the Confederate army, and the third also appears to have deserted to the Confederate army, but the record is incomplete.[7] The Widow Bixby attempted to con the federal government into paying for her alleged loss.

Regardless of the true facts concerning Mrs. Bixby and her sons, Abraham Lincoln was an innocent victim of her fraud. He had been shown documentation suggesting her five sons were killed, and wrote his letter out of sincere empathy for what he believed was a grieving mother. Interestingly, he may also be the victim of identity theft. In 1940, a startling claim emerged that Lincoln was not the author of the letter. Rather his secretary, John Hay, was the author. Lincoln merely signed the letter.

The Bixby letter is often cited as being among Lincoln's greater literary writings, ranking it along with the Gettysburg Address and his second inaugural address. It received special attention in 1998 when Steven Spielberg added it to the movie script of *Saving Private Ryan*. Harve Presnell, portraying George C. Marshall, then army chief of staff, read the letter on-screen after learning of the deaths of three Ryan brothers in World War II. The reading introduced a new generation of Americans to the poignant letter.

The original letter is missing, believed destroyed by Mrs. Bix-

Michael Tobin facsimile of the Bixby letter produced in 1891.
Edward Steers Jr. collection.

by. A facsimile of the letter appeared in 1891 that was later ruled an artist's copy when it was traced to Michael Tobin, a New York dealer in prints and engravings. Tobin employed an artist to engrave the facsimile based on Lincoln's known handwriting. Tobin sold souvenir copies of the letter for $2.[8] Over the years, the copies have reappeared from time to time, fooling people into believing it to be the long lost original of Lincoln's famous letter.

The claim that Lincoln's secretary John Hay authored the original letter first appeared in 1940 in an autobiographical memoir by Columbia University's president, Nicholas Murray Butler. In his autobiography Butler related a third-person account of an incident in which the British statesman John Morley visited President Theodore Roosevelt in the White House. Morley noted the framed facsimile of the Bixby letter hanging in the guest bedroom. Roosevelt told Morley how much he admired Lincoln's letter. Several days later Morley visited with then Secretary of State John Hay and told him about Roosevelt's admiration of the Bixby letter. "After a brief silence, John Hay told Morley that he had himself written the Bixby letter." Hay asked Morley not to mention this to anyone until after Hay's death. Morley kept the secret until seven years after Hay's death, when he told the story to Nicholas Murray Butler, swearing Butler to secrecy until Morley died.[9]

Thus we have Hay telling Morley, who told Butler, who told the world in his autobiography. Hay, it seems, broke his own secrecy oath at least twice more. He told American journalist W. C. Brownell, who in turn told the editor of the *New York Times*, Rollo Ogden. And lastly, Hay told the American ambassador to the United Kingdom, Walter Hines Page, who then told Lady Strafford, who told the Reverend G. A. Jackson. Thus we have a string of third- and fourth-person accounts, but no account directly from Hay claiming to have written the letter. These third- and fourth-person claims are interesting, but they hardly offer sufficient proof to overcome what history has accepted for over 150 years.

Hay was an accomplished writer in his own right. A graduate of Brown University, Hay donated most of his papers to the university following his death in 1905. Among the papers is a scrapbook containing many of the poems and articles he wrote during his lifetime. In researching a book on Hay, Lincoln historian Michael Burlingame came across the scrapbook.[10] In it he found a clipping of the Bixby letter. Burlingame found it strange that Hay would choose to paste a clipping of the Bixby letter among his own writings if he were not the author. On further research, he noticed that the word "beguile" ap-

John Hay. National Archives and Records Administration.

pears in none of Lincoln's other writings, but is found among several of Hay's works. Burlingame concluded that this discovery, when taken together with the early-twentieth-century accounts, supports the claim that Hay, not Lincoln, authored the famous letter. Burlingame is quick to point out that such a conclusion in no way diminishes Lincoln's reputation as a literary genius.[11]

While Burlingame's conclusion has gained a footing among a few Lincoln scholars, it really warrants a more intensive examination of the question. We are all creatures of habit. That is to say, we find certain comfort in repetition, doing things the same way. Even when we try to be different we often give ourselves away by peculiar traits that reflect our habits. This is especially true when we are alone, with no one to worry about except ourselves. Few actions are more solitary than writing. In writing we withdraw into our own mind and concentrate on the single act of composing our thoughts and transcribing them to paper (or a computer screen in this particular instance). Thus, we are characterized by certain patterns of style. Even when we attempt to disguise our writing we betray ourselves by letting our style habits show through.

Among the many areas of scholarship is one known simply as "text analysis" or "linguistic analysis." Such analysts look at writing in regard to words, rhetoric, punctuation, and style. They analyze the internal evidence of composition and, if they are really good at it, are able to identify an anonymous writer with reasonable accuracy. Among the few who excel in text analysis are Joe Nickell and Jean Pival. Nickell, a "forensic linguist" by training (University of Kentucky) and a senior research fellow for the Committee for Skeptical Inquiry and associate dean of the Center for Inquiry, has challenged various historical, paranormal, and forensic mysteries, as well as myths and hoaxes in general. Among his many targets are the famous poem "A Visit from St. Nicholas" (more popularly known as "The Night before Christmas"), the purported diary of Jack the Ripper, and Abraham Lincoln's celebrated Bixby letter. Jean Pival is a professor specializing in English linguistics and rhetoric at the University of Kentucky and the author of several books on linguistics.

Six years before Burlingame's discovery of the Hay scrapbook and his announcement to the historical community, these two experts in linguistics analyzed the Bixby letter in an effort to determine its author.[12] Nickell summarized his analysis in a table published in the *Lincoln Herald,* comparing Lincoln's phraseology. The following table from Nickell's article in the *Herald* shows the results of his analysis. In addition, Nickell noted that Lincoln's use of the word "tender," meaning "to offer," was characteristic of his writing and is absent from Hay's writings. In the Bixby letter Lincoln writes: "tendering you. . . ." Examples from Lincoln's other writings include: "tender you my sincere thanks," "that it was tendered you," "so kindly tendered," "so generously tendered," "cordially tendered me," "tendered this invitation," and "the tendered honor."[13] Lincoln's choice of this word in place of "offer" is characteristic of his style. It stems from Lincoln's legal training, where "tender" is commonly used. Nickell also noted the use throughout Lincoln's writings of alliteration for rhetorical effect. Again, this form of style sets Lincoln and Hay apart. In the Bixby letter one finds: "beguile you from the grief," "assuage the anguish," and "loved and lost." This same writing style can be found throughout Lincoln's other writings: "blows and bloodshed," "lamp of liberty," "scorned and scouted."[14]

Professor Jean Pival analyzed the Bixby letter along with other writings of both men at the request of Nickell. In her analysis she wrote: "There is more than a generational difference in their [Lincoln and Hay] syntax and vocabulary.... Lincoln was a certified lawyer who practiced law for over twenty years.... Legal usages and formal argument structures abound even in his personal letters, while Hay's writings show little or no influence of such background. Whereas Hay's personal writings are full of the slang contemporary

Table I. A Comparison of Lincoln Phraseology

Gettysburg Address	*Other Lincoln Writings*
It is altogether fitting and proper	it is altogether befitting (VI, 139); it is most proper (VI, 134); It has seemed to me fit and proper (IX, 152)
... the unfinished work which they who fought here have thus far so nobly advanced	the blood they have so nobly shed (XI, 125); to advance the great cause (VI, 130)
that government of the people, by the people, for the people, shall not perish from the earth.	a government of the people by the same people (VI, 304); will endure forever (V, 49).

Table II. A Comparison of the Bixby Text with Lincoln Writings

Bixby Letter	*Lincoln Writings*
Dear Madam:	My Dear Madam (X, 253)
I have been shown in the files of the War Department a statement of the Adjutant-General of Massachusetts that you are the mother of five sons	I see your dispatch to the Secretary of War (XI, 50); There have recently reached the War Department, and thence been laid before me, from Missouri, three communications (IX, 186)
who have died gloriously on the field of battle.	too weak (I, 42); fruitless every attempt (I, 43); what so humble an individual as myself chose to say (V, 36);
which should attempt to beguile you from the grief	which might divert your mind (I, 183); no intrusion upon the sacredness of your sorrow (VI, 288)
of a loss so overwhelming.	of a work so vast (IX, 215); of a citizen so venerable (X, 276); support so unanimously given (X, 101)
But I cannot refrain from tendering to you the consolation that may be found in the thanks of the Republic they died to save.	I tender to you . . . the thanks of the nation (X, 213); the nation's sympathy (XII, 14); those who here gave their lives that that nation might live (IX, 209–10).
I pray that our heavenly Father may assuage	I pray God (X, 170); prayers to our Father in Heaven (X, 216); invoke the influence of his Holy Spirit to subdue (IX, 33); more sorrow assuaged (I, 208)
the anguish of your bereavement	the sad bereavement you mention (X, 330); the depths of affliction (V, 255)

Bixby Letter	Lincoln Writings
and leave you only the cherished memory	its beloved history and cherished memories (VII, 273)
of the loved and lost	from these honored dead (IX, 210); The death-scenes of those we love (I, 186); loved ones lost (I, 291)
and the solemn pride that must be yours.	may justly pride themselves (VI, 329); solemn awe (I, 209); a matter of honor and pride (I, 266).

Source: Nickell, "Lincoln's Bixby Letter," 138–139.

to his youth, Lincoln's letters are more formal in character—even old-fashioned."[15]

Burlingame made a point of the fact that the word "beguile" appears only in the Bixby letter and nowhere else in Lincoln's writings[16] while it appears several times in Hay's writings.[17] Pival, however, points out that the two men use the word differently. In the Bixby letter, "beguile" is used in the Elizabethan sense of diverting or deceiving, while Hay uses the word as meaning "to charm or entice." Pival concludes that Lincoln is the author of the Bixby letter, writing, "There is too much stylistic evidence to believe otherwise."[18] As to using the word "beguile" only once, Lincoln also used the word "disenthrall" only once, and then in his famous second annual address to the Congress on December 1, 1862.[19] This fact lessens Burlingame's "sole use" argument for the word "beguile."*

There is one other stylistic clue in support of Lincoln's authorship of the letter. It involves what Lincoln once referred to as "this little fellow." It is the adverb "so." Unlike Hay, and other writers of his

---

*The words "abideth" and "aberrations" also appear only once in Lincoln's writings.

generation, Lincoln had a special fondness for this word. He used it twice in the Bixby letter: "a loss so overwhelming," and "so costly a sacrifice." In his hallmark piece, the Gettysburg Address, he used the adverb three times: "so conceived and so dedicated," and "so nobly advanced." This unusual usage was peculiar to Lincoln, revealing a distinctive literary signature.[20]

Aside from such scholarly analyses, which the majority of us are unable to perform, there is one last piece of evidence that assigns the authorship of the letter to Lincoln. In a series of letters exchanged between Lincoln's son, Robert Todd Lincoln, and Isaac Markens, a journalist and author,[21] Robert Lincoln wrote that he had a special interest in the letter. Not in who wrote the letter, but in what happened to it. Markens had raised the question with Robert as to Hay's authorship of the letter. Markens had no doubt Lincoln wrote the letter, and sought Robert's reassurance. Robert wrote back to Markens, "Your suggestion that neither Nicolay or Hay [Lincoln's two secretaries] probably had any special knowledge of the letter at the time is correct. *Hay himself told me so* [emphasis added]; when I took the matter up Nicolay had died and it was he who had compiled the collection of papers [Lincoln's official correspondence published by Nicolay and Hay]."[22] Robert also stated that when he showed the facsimile letter to Hay during one of their meetings, Hay knew nothing about the facsimile and gave no indication that he had been the author of the original letter.[23]

These statements by Robert Lincoln, although hearsay in the legal sense, suggest that Hay himself had no knowledge of the letter at the time it was written. Whether Burlingame was unaware of earlier studies by Nickell and Pival on style, or of the letter from Robert Lincoln to Isaac Markens, is not known. In his articles he mentions neither, giving no citation to them in his endnotes. If Burlingame was aware of these earlier sources, he should have countered their arguments and informed his readers why their discoveries should be dismissed. This evidence certainly deserves consideration con-

Robert Todd Lincoln.
Library of Congress.

cerning the question of who authored the famous letter. Those who believe Hay wrote the letter have an obligation to refute the conclusions of those who believe Lincoln to be the author.

N-Gram Analysis

Most recently, the question of Lincoln's authorship of the Bixby letter received a new challenge. This challenge was more serious than previous ones. At a symposium at Ford's Theatre on March 16, 2019, Michael Burlingame again told his audience of his conclusion that Hay authored the Bixby letter. He bolstered his claim by mentioning a new technology designed to analyze short documents that could determine the probability of authorship. A group of researchers in Birmingham, England, had analyzed the Bixby letter along with several documents known to be written by Abraham Lincoln and others known to be authored by John Hay.[24] The Bixby letter contains only 139 words, making it something of a challenge to forensic linguists.

After analyzing the Bixby letter against several documents by both writers, the Birmingham group concluded that Hay was the author of the Bixby letter to a "ninety percent" certainty. Their analysis, Burlingame said, "settled the question" once and for all.[25]

The new technique is known as "N-gram tracing." The assumption in linguistic analysis is that writers have a style of writing that can be recognized by determining the probability of character and word sequence. It is similar to the stylistic approach to forensic analysis of writing except that it relies on using probability analysis to assess authorship.

N-gram analysis, in its simplest terms, is a method for establishing a mathematical probability of authorship for an unknown (or challenged) document based on letter and word sequence. It is a mathematical theory of communication. After applying N-gram analysis to a text, one can state whether the suspected author is the producer of the document with a 100 percent probability, or with a 0 percent probability, or any number in between. It is a conclusion based on statistical analysis of the internal content of the document. How does it work?

"N" stands for number; "gram" stands for grammar. N-grams are combinations of items of length N that occur in the subject text (corpus). N may consist of letters, syllables, words, or phrases. In the case of words, the N-gram process predicts the probability of the next word in a sequence based on the previous word and the style of the author. In the case of a two-word analysis, referred to as a bigram, the word San is more likely to be followed by Diego or Francisco than by dog or house. This type of analysis can be done for three words (trigrams) or four words (4 grams), and so on. After analyzing an entire text one can assign a probability that it was written by author Y based on a similar analysis of texts that are known to be written by author Y.

One of the problems for this type of analysis concerns the size of the text and the number of texts in the analyzed pool. The longer the text, and the larger the pool, the better. It should be obvious that as the text gets smaller and smaller, the reliability of the analysis decreases, eventually approaching zero. The Bixby letter consists of only 139 words, a very small sample size. Normally, a text this small would not lend itself to N-gram analysis. Jack Grieve and his fellow researchers claim to have overcome this limitation with their own form of N-gram analysis, which they call "N-gram tracing." They concluded with a high degree of probability that John Hay, and not Abraham Lincoln, authored the Bixby letter.

On the face of it, it is hard to see how such a limited number of words can give a reasonably high degree of probability. This question on document length is specifically addressed by Thomas Proisl and his coworkers in a study published in 2018 resulting from their presentation at the Eleventh International Conference held in Miyazaki, Japan.[26] In their study, Proisl and his colleagues asked two questions: "To what extent does authorship attribution accuracy depend on the length of the disputed text, and the size of the corpus against which it is compared?" and, "Is there a minimum text length below which results become unreliable?"[27] These are precisely the questions that need to be answered before accepting N-gram analysis of the Bixby letter.

Proisl and his colleagues found that the method of N-gram tracing performed "rather poorly for very short texts, where they have to attribute, for example, a 250-word fragment to one of 25 possible authors with only 500 words of comparison text per author."[28] In their conclusion, the authors state: "N-gram tracing requires text lengths of 1,000–3,000 words, and a large enough comparison corpus to achieve an acceptable accuracy of 80%."[29] The Bixby letter falls well below this minimum requirement of 1,000–3,000 words that Proisl and his coworkers suggest are necessary for accurate attribution. These results throw the conclusion of Grieve and his colleagues that N-gram tracing shows Hay to be the author of the Bixby letter into doubt.

What appears to be a flaw in the Grieve et al. analysis comes from their choice of documents analyzed. In the case of Lincoln, all of his writings after May 1860 were excluded, presumably because some might have been written by Hay. Hay's body of work was limited to only those documents written after May 1860. This would seem to compare apples and oranges. Certainly Lincoln's writings during his presidency may better reflect his style of writing as found in the Bixby letter, which, after all, was written after May 1860.

The one thing that N-gram analysis cannot do that is important to forensic analysis is evaluate the meaning of words peculiar to an individual. The use of the word "tender" by Lincoln is one example. "Beguile" is another. N-gram analysis cannot make this distinction between meanings.

While Burlingame believes the controversy over the authorship of the Bixby letter is settled, it appears to be still open. Burlingame's conclusions as to authorship may have some merit, but they are not conclusive. If one is making extraordinary claims, one needs extraordinary evidence. Until more definitive evidence emerges, Lincoln still holds claim to having written the letter to Mrs. Bixby.

Abe and Ann

He Loves Me, He Loves Me Not

For better or for worse, the alleged love affair between Abraham Lincoln and Ann Rutledge is here to stay. While controversial among academic historians who continue to argue over its veracity, the general public needs no convincing; Abe loved Ann. And why not? What is more interesting than a secret love affair that ends in tragedy? Shakespeare would stand up and cheer.

Abraham Lincoln is surrounded by controversy and myth. A great emancipator or white supremacist; a boyhood filled with mirth and joy or misery's child; he saved the Union, but caused the war; gay or straight, you can fool some of the people all of the time, and all of the people some of the time, but you can't fool all of the people all of the time. Sorry, but it appears someone fooled us. That last little ditty does not come from Abraham Lincoln; it comes from P. T. Barnum.[1] Researching and writing about Abraham Lincoln is more fun than curling.

In a limited survey of twenty-six eminent Lincoln historians, the vote is evenly divided; thirteen believe a love affair existed, while thirteen do not. A few have even changed sides over the years, flip-flopping in their views. The controversy centers on a group of informants, or witnesses, who rely on their memory after some thirty years—misty memories of a time and place long past.

Abe and Ann did exist, and they both resided in a small community at a time in their young lives when amorous hormones flooded the emotions. And it all took place in the pioneer village of New Salem, Illinois.

Ann Rutledge being waited on by Abraham Lincoln in the Berry and Lincoln store in New Salem. From a postcard, Edward Steers Jr. collection.

The Berry-Lincoln store in 1922. Blackhawk Hiking Club Album, Edward Steers Jr. collection.

In the Beginning

In 1828, John Hanks, Nancy Hanks Lincoln's first cousin and Abraham Lincoln's first cousin once removed, left Indiana for the rich prairie land of Illinois. John had lived with the Lincoln family in Indiana for four years, from 1822 to 1826.[2] John had decided that Illinois was preferable to Indiana, not the least reason for which was its rich prairie soil. Two years later, the feared disease known as "milk sickness" once again spread its killing wings over the Indiana communities around Gentryville and Pigeon Creek, where Thomas and his family lived. Thomas had lost his wife, Nancy, to the disease in 1818, and he was not anxious to lose any more of his family. At John Hanks's encouragement, Thomas decided to move to the Decatur region of Illinois.

The land was fertile, affordable, and most of all free from the dreaded milk sickness. John Hanks selected a tract along the Sangamon River for his friend and set about cutting trees and hewing them into cabin logs in anticipation of Thomas's arrival. The migration would be the fifth for Thomas since his marriage to Nancy in 1806. His restlessness was common among frontier people.

This time Thomas's migration would include his second wife, Sarah Bush Johnston Lincoln, his wife's three children, his son Abraham, and the families of Dennis Hanks and Squire Hall, a total of thirteen people. The trip took fifteen days, from March 1 to March 15, and covered two hundred miles in freezing, miserable weather. The Lincolns entered the state of Illinois by crossing the Wabash River at Vincennes, Indiana. The caravan consisted of thirteen people, two ox-drawn wagons, one horse-drawn wagon, and a small dog. It crossed the river into Illinois on March 6, 1830.

William Herndon, Lincoln's law partner, related an incident told to him by Lincoln that occurred during the crossing of the Wabash River into Indiana involving his little dog:

One day the little fellow fell behind and failed to catch up till af-

Lincoln Trail Memorial designed and carved by Nellie Verne Walker. Erected in 1938, the memorial sits at the western edge of the Lincoln Memorial Bridge over the Wabash River. Photograph by Edward Steers Jr.

ter they had crossed the stream. Missing him, they looked back, and there, on the opposite bank, he stood whining and jumping about in great distress. The water was running over the broken edges of the ice, and the poor animal was afraid to cross. It would not pay to turn the oxen and wagon back and ford the stream again in order to recover a dog, and so the majority, in their anxiety to move forward, decided to go on without him. "But I could not endure the idea of abandoning even a dog," related Lincoln. "Pulling off shoes and socks I waded across the stream and triumphantly returned with the shivering animal under my arm. His frantic leaps of joy and other evidences of a dog's gratitude amply repaid me for all the exposure I had undergone."[3]

Arriving in Illinois, Lincoln set about helping his father and John Hanks construct a new cabin about ten miles from Decatur. Finishing just in time for the coming snows of winter, the family settled in and waited for spring. That winter a major blizzard struck the region, leaving a deep blanket of snow covering the prairie. When spring came, Lincoln, having recently celebrated his twenty-second birthday, bid his father and stepmother good-bye. He had been a dutiful son long enough, and now it was time to strike out on his own. Once again, John Hanks lured a Lincoln into adventure, only this time it was Abraham, not Thomas, who was lured.

Hanks had contracted with Denton Offutt, a mercurial entrepreneur from the village of Springfield, to construct a flatboat and transport his merchandise down the Illinois and Mississippi Rivers to New Orleans. It was a challenging task, but one which Lincoln had done three years earlier when living in Indiana.[4] Hanks asked Lincoln and his stepbrother, John D. Johnston, if they were interested in joining with him. The two men jumped at the opportunity of travel and money.

Offutt was in many ways Abraham Lincoln's savior. At the very least, he was the young Lincoln's door to the future. He would become Lincoln's employer in the flatboat venture, and later Lincoln would work as Offutt's clerk in a New Salem store. Lincoln was also fortunate to have John Hanks as a family member and close friend. In 1866, Hanks gave a lengthy and illustrative account of his days with Lincoln in an interview with William Herndon. He told Herndon of the river trip that would eventually land Lincoln in the pioneer village of New Salem: "Offutt came to my house in Feb'y 1831, and wanted to hire me to run a flat boat for him—Saying that he had heard that I was quite a flatboatman in Ky: he wanted me to go badly. I went & saw Abe & Jno Johnson—Abes step brother—introduced Offutt to them. We made an engagement with Offutt at 50 [cents] per day and $60 to make the trip to New Orleans."[5]

Hanks agreed. Rounding up his two partners, he set out for Springfield, where Offutt had promised to have a flatboat loaded

Abraham Lincoln flatboats on the Mississippi River. From Noah Brooks, *Abraham Lincoln: A Biography for Young People*, 1888.

with cargo waiting for them. When the three men arrived in Springfield, however, they found Offutt in the Buckhorn Tavern deep into liquor, and no flatboat. He had failed to have a flatboat waiting for the men as promised. Somewhat chagrined, Offutt offered to pay the men $12 a month to build the flatboat. Although it set back the planned trip by six weeks, it proved a blessing for the men. It was extra money in their pockets.

Led by Hanks, the three men set out for a patch of federal land four miles north of Springfield, where they found ample free trees to use for their boat. After felling the trees, they floated them down the Sangamon River to a sawmill at Sangamo Town, where they had the logs cut into timber.

Over the next two weeks the men worked long, hard hours constructing a huge flatboat eighty feet long and eighteen feet wide. By mid-April they were ready to launch their wooden ark. One observer noted, "When the boat was completed it was shoved into the river, [which] created something of a stir in town."[6] It seemed as if the whole community had looked on as the men went about building their boat, waiting for the day it would be launched.

Once launched, the seaworthy craft, along with the four men, now captained by Denton Offutt, began its sixteen-hundred-mile trip from Sangamo Town to New Orleans. Barely underway, the flatboat and her cargo experienced near disaster. At the pioneer village of New Salem, just twenty-four miles northwest of Springfield, Offutt's flatboat became caught amidships on a cofferdam while attempting to slip over it. Two years earlier, two enterprising young men had received a license to build a grist and sawmill on the Sangamon River. They diverted water from the river to their mill by way of a dam. The dam proved an obstruction to the normal navigation of the river for vessels the size of Offutt's flatboat.

The entrapped boat, with its bow elevated over the dam and stern lowered behind it, began to take on water. The situation threatened to destroy much of the cargo if the boat continued to founder. Offutt, inexperienced at such matters, was flustered, not knowing what to do. It was at this point that Lincoln took charge. He not only saved the boat and its cargo, but changed his own life in a way unimaginable at that critical moment.

Unloading most of the cargo to an empty boat nearby, Lincoln waded ashore and borrowed an augur from the village cooper, Henry Onstott. With the cargo unloaded, the water transferred from the stern to the bow area overhanging the dam. Lincoln augured a hole in the bottom, allowing the water to drain out, after which he plugged the hole. The lightened boat easily slipped over the dam undamaged save for a plugged hole in its bow. Lincoln's quick thinking had saved the day, and Offutt's cargo.

While all this was taking place, the entire village of New Salem gathered along the bank of the river and watched with some amusement as events unfolded. The crowd was sure the boat would lose its cargo and end in disaster. The lanky twenty-two-year-old made a positive impression on the crowd. "That fellow was a clever lad," they said.

The incident had delayed the trip by a full day, but during the unloading and reloading of the flatboat, Offutt had a chance to look over the village. Ever the entrepreneur, he instantly saw an opportunity. Here was a place where he could do business. And in the rescue of his cargo he found just the man to run it. As the flatboat shoved off from the New Salem shore and continued its long journey to New Orleans, Offutt decided he would return to the village and bring the man who saved his cargo with him. He would build a store and pay Lincoln to run it.

New Salem

Having completed the job of delivering Denton Offutt's cargo to New Orleans, Lincoln, now on his own for the first time, returned to the village of New Salem. Offutt had purchased a building there and hired Lincoln to be his clerk. When Lincoln arrived in the village in July 1831, Offutt, as usual, was nowhere to be found. Lincoln knew he would eventually arrive, and until then he reconnoitered the village and "rapidly made acquaintances and friends," something he was good at.[7]

The village of New Salem was only two years old when the young Lincoln arrived. New Salem sprang from the vision of two men, James Rutledge and John Cameron. After failing to build a gristmill along Concord Creek in Sangamon County in 1826 just seven miles north of New Salem due to inadequate water flow, Rutledge and Cameron received permission from the Illinois state legislature to build a dam along the Sangamon River. The Sangamon was a large, rapidly flowing body of water easily suited to supply power to a mill. The two men built their homes on a bluff overlooking the river and then set about building a milldam to power their saw and gristmill. By the fall of 1829 the mill was ready for business. Its success soon

The Rutledge Tavern, where Lincoln first met Ann Rutledge. Photograph by Edward Steers Jr.

attracted other entrepreneurs who, hoping to take advantage of the growing number of farmers who came to the mill, built a store, which was soon followed by a "grocery" or saloon. Farmers bringing their grain or lumber to the mill now had a place to buy sundries and to gather and drink while waiting for their lumber to be sawed or their grain to be milled.

By the fall of 1829 a village plat had been laid out with fifty-six lots separated in near equal halves by a road running down the middle. Lots sold for $7 to $12 and were quickly snapped up. Samuel Hill and John McNamar, two early residents, opened a store and were soon followed by Henry Onstott, who built a home and cooperage at the far end of town. These early residents were soon joined by a doctor, a blacksmith, and a schoolteacher.

As the village grew over the succeeding months, James Rutledge converted his home into a tavern, taking advantage of the numerous people who traveled to his mill. By the time Lincoln floated into New Salem in the spring of 1831, the village had grown to just over one hundred people and twenty-two log structures. It boasted a mill, two stores, a post office, a carding mill, a blacksmith, two doctors, a cooperage, a school, and a saloon.

When Lincoln arrived, he first boarded and took several of his meals at the Rutledge Tavern. James and Mary Ann Rutledge had nine children, the third oldest being a girl named Ann who was born in 1813. She was eighteen years old when the twenty-two-year-old Lincoln arrived in New Salem. By all descriptions, Ann was the belle of the village. Many years after her death in 1835, neighbors described her to William Herndon, who was gathering information for a proposed biography of Lincoln. "This young lady was a woman of Exquisite beauty.... She had a gentle & kind a heart as an angel—full of love—kindness—sympathy."[8] Her physical description was equally complimentary, "Eyes blue, large & Expressive—fair complexion—Sandy or light auburn hair—face rather round—outlines beautiful—about 5-4 in—weight about 120-130."[9] By any measure, Ann was a prize catch in a frontier village of only one hundred people.

Lincoln, on the other hand, did not fare nearly as well: "[He] was six feet four inches high in his stockings. Stoop shouldered, his legs were long, feet large; arms long, longer than any man I ever knew."[10] "He wore flax & tow linen pantaloons [a coarse linen] I think about 5 inches too short in the legs showing most of his shinbones and frequently he had but one suspender—a straw hat and potmetal boots [made of coarse, black leather]."[11] The description is one of a gangly rube with little to offer any woman.

But Lincoln had other qualities that made people soon forget his appearance. Nathaniel Branson, a Petersburg lawyer, described Lincoln's character in a letter to William Herndon: "Lincoln was very agreeable in company and everybody liked him. Was always full of life & fun—always cheerful—always had a story to tell. Knew every man, woman & child for miles around—was very fond of children.

Was fond of cats—would take one and turn it on its back & talk to it for half an hour at a time . . . I never in my life saw him out of humor. He never got angry."[12] The two young villagers seemed complete opposites in their physical traits, but one thing they did share was a love of learning. It was this love that drew them together first as friends, and later as lovers, or so some would claim.

When Lincoln arrived in New Salem, Ann Rutledge was engaged to one of New Salem's more successful occupants, John McNamar, Samuel Hill's mercantile partner.[13] Hill and McNamar ran a store in the heart of the village. McNamar had fallen in love with the young Ann, and proposed marriage to her. She accepted, and the two were soon known throughout the village as lovers who were engaged to marry.

In late 1832, one year after Lincoln had arrived, McNamar decided to return to his family home in Ohio, New York, to settle his father's debts. He confessed to Ann that his real name was McNeil and that he assumed the name McNamar to cover his trail when he left home to make his fortune. He wanted anonymity for reasons never fully explained. Now that he had acquired a sufficient amount of money, he would return home and provide for his parents' welfare, after which he would return to New Salem and marry Ann.[14]

Following his arrival in New York, McNamar found his father critically ill. The old man soon died, and McNamar was left to settle family affairs. The two lovers corresponded regularly at first, but McNamar's letters became fewer and fewer as time passed. One year turned into two, then two into three. Toward the latter part of his stay in New York his letters to Ann stopped completely, and for several months Ann heard nothing from her fiancé. It was assumed he would never return to New Salem, leaving his engagement to Ann in an uncertain state. But McNamar did return to New Salem in August 1835, only to find his beloved Ann had died two weeks earlier from typhoid fever. However, the story doesn't end there. It was just beginning.

Within a few weeks of Lincoln's death in April 1865, his law partner of twenty-one years, William Herndon, decided to write a biography of the true Lincoln, or, as he said, "the true life of Mr. L." John Locke Scripps, a journalist and author who wrote an early biography of Lincoln for the 1860 presidential campaign, wrote to Herndon on learning that Herndon was about to write his own: "I am glad you design giving us something about Lincoln. Your long acquaintance and close association with him must have given you a clearer insight into his character than other men obtained."[15]

While Herndon probably knew more about the intimate Lincoln than anyone else, he was not content to write solely from his own experiences with his famous partner. Herndon set out to gather as much personal information on Lincoln as he could from those who knew him, and who lived in his presence throughout his life. Herndon began writing and interviewing as many of these people as he could find. His letters were filled with questions (interrogatories, as his subjects often referred to his questions) probing every aspect of Lincoln's life. He would write to one of his informants and direct them to "Get all the facts & write to me." They did, more than 250 people in all. This was a monumental task Herndon had undertaken, and while much of what he gathered is subject to controversy, his research has given us the most complete and far-reaching set of accounts of Lincoln's early years. In fact, on most subjects it is the only information we have.

Among Herndon's informants is a group of people from Lincoln's New Salem years. Many of these people knew Herndon and were willing to answer all of his questions, some with great embellishment. Today, we are fortunate to have the bulk of Herndon's interviews, which were collected and annotated in a single volume by historians Douglas L. Wilson and Rodney O. Davis.[16] Sifting through their reminiscences is not always easy, but it is a necessary task if we are to make sense of Lincoln's early life.

Abe and Ann

William Herndon. Library of Congress.

Long before he wrote Lincoln's biography, Herndon became Lincoln's oral biographer. He prepared a lecture on his partner and delivered it on November 16, 1866, to a full house in Lincoln's hometown of Springfield. Looking over the audience, Herndon paused a moment for dramatic effect, then began his lecture with these stunning words: "Lincoln loved Ann Rutledge better than his own life."[17] With that opening sentence Herndon launched one of the most poetic, and controversial, love stories in American history.

When Herndon began his research shortly after Lincoln's death, he had no idea of the claims by some of Lincoln's New Salem neighbors that Lincoln had fallen in love with the village beauty and had become engaged only to see his love die tragically in the bloom of life. Devastated, the young Lincoln fell into deep despair. So serious was his depression that his neighbors feared for his life.

The Lincoln-Rutledge love affair was a heart-wrenching story, yet beautiful in its poignancy. Herndon's lecture describing Lincoln's first love, and its tragic end, stirred bitter controversy at the time. Mary Todd Lincoln was still alive, and Herndon's claim that Ann Rutledge was Lincoln's first and only love was viewed as a dagger thrust into the heart of the grieving widow. There had been bitter animosity between Herndon and Mary Lincoln while her husband was alive. The two had a falling out, and she forbid his ever entering her Springfield home, calling him a "a dirty dog."[18]

Controversial at the time, the alleged love affair is equally controversial today among academic scholars who have chosen sides over whether he loved her or loved her not. Eminent Lincoln scholars such as James G. Randall and John Y. Simon fall on rival sides of this story's fault line. Like most controversies concerning Lincoln, each side selectively cherry-picks the evidence, and there is plenty of evidence to choose from on either side of the question.

That Ann Rutledge was engaged to John McNamar when Lincoln arrived in New Salem in July 1831 is true. That McNamar left New Salem to return to his family's home in New York in the fall of 1832, and failed to return until August 1835, two weeks after Ann's death, is true. That Lincoln suffered some sort of depression following Ann's death is also true. What happened during those three years of McNamar's absence is the crux of the story.

Those who embrace the legend point to the testimony that is consistent. Over a dozen individuals repeat the same basic facts of the story: a courtship took place resulting in an engagement that was never consummated due to Ann's death. This was followed by her lover falling into deep despair, rendering him functionless.

James G. Randall, recognized by many as the dean of early Lincoln scholars, attacked the story of Abe and Ann head on. He was able to convince most of the historical academy that the story was nothing more than a myth created by Herndon through his informants. The thrust of Randall's attack is aimed at the memory of Herndon's informants that he characterizes as "dim and misty," the untrustworthy memories of old people of a time and place far away, too far away to be reliable.

Before discussing the evidence both for and against a romance and engagement, one must consider what everyone accepts as true. First, everyone agrees that Ann was engaged to John McNamar during the period Lincoln lived in New Salem up to the time of Ann's death (1831–1835). Second, everyone agrees that Lincoln showed signs of some form of unusual depression following Ann's death. All of the claims about a romantic relationship beyond these two accepted facts are arguable. It is important to note, however, that none of the informants claiming a romantic relationship also claim to have seen any signs of courtship or expressions of love, such as holding hands or kissing.

The most credible proponents supporting a romance are historians Douglas L. Wilson, coeditor with Rodney O. Davis of *Herndon's Informants*, and John Y. Simon, editor of the Ulysses S. Grant Papers and a former professor of history at Southern Illinois University. The statures of these two academicians in the field of history add credibility to the question of a possible romance. Credibility, but not proof. Wilson relies on the testimony of twenty-four informants who responded to a series of questions posed by William Herndon, most between 1865 and 1866, while Simon relies on select testimony of a few informants, and on Lincoln's behavior following Ann's death.

In Wilson's analysis, out of the twenty-four informants, three claim to have learned of a romantic involvement directly from one or both of the individuals. This means that twenty-one of the informants relied on hearsay or secondhand information; they had heard of the alleged relationship from someone else, but had not witnessed it themselves. They had no firsthand knowledge of a relationship. It is this second category that gives many historians a problem. Their testimony comes thirty or more years after the alleged events occurred, leading to challenges of memory reliability over such a long period. While all twenty-four agree there was a romantic relationship, they often differ in the details, which might be expected over such a long period of time, and most important, none claims to have ever seen any signs of romantic behavior on the couple's part. This differing of details is often used against the witnesses' reliability by those who do not accept the romance.

The principal informant supporting a romance is Robert Rutledge (1819–1881), the younger brother of Ann. Robert was sixteen years old at the time of Ann's death, old enough to recognize the signs of romance, but he gave no testimony from his own personal experience, suggesting that he was unaware of any relationship. Robert agreed to query other members of his family for their recollections, including Ann's mother, Mary Ann Rutledge. Who should know better than Ann's own family, and her mother in particular?

Robert Rutledge corresponded several times with William Herndon (nine letters in all),[19] each time answering specific questions that Herndon had posed. Robert consulted his mother, Mary Ann, and his older brother, John, but neither Mary Ann nor John admitted to Herndon directly of any romantic relationship between Ann and Lincoln; that was left for Robert to describe.

Robert began his long letter of November 1, 1866, to Herndon:

> You make some pertinent inquiries concerning my sister and the relations, which existed between her and Mr. Lincoln. Mr. Lincoln paid his addresses to Ann, continued his visits and intentions regularly and those resulted in an engagement to marry, conditional to an honorable release from the contract with McNamar. There is no kind of doubt as to the existence of this engagement. David Rutledge[20] urged Ann to consummate it, but she refused until such time as she could see McNamar—inform him of the change in her feelings, and seek an honorable release.[21]

This statement by Robert is a little disconcerting. As Robert claims to know nothing of a romantic relationship between Ann and Lincoln, he presumably queried his mother and older brother, and cousin, McGrady Rutledge, and yet he does not mention them by name nor does he relay any specifics they might have said to him. He merely summarizes what he heard. Of all the people Ann might confide in, her mother is the most obvious, and the one we would really like to hear from.

It appears Herndon never contacted her, or if he did, she did not respond. This leaves Robert's statement one of hearsay, and questionable as to who informed him. Someone told him that his brother David urged his sister to marry Lincoln. David died in 1842, twenty-four years before Robert's letter. So, this alleged statement by David was passed through at least two people twenty-four years after the fact. From a historian's point of view, Robert's testimony is hearsay at best and lacking in important detail.

Lewis Gannett, an American writer and editor of C. A. Tripp's *The Intimate World of Abraham Lincoln*, points out in his article on the alleged romance that David Rutledge was "the only cited witness" by his brother Robert, and David was dead.[22] Gannett dismisses Robert's testimony, writing: "Since Robert did not quote his mother, Mary, or his brother, John M., we cannot know with certainty that either one actually affirmed an engagement, or indeed whether either had anything at all to say about a romance."[23]

There are three witnesses found in *Herndon's Informants* who claim they were told directly, either by Lincoln or Ann, of the love affair: Isaac Cogdal, Mentor Graham, and James McGrady Rutledge. All three men had lived in New Salem at one time, and all three knew Lincoln and Ann. Direct witnesses are what historians seek. Assuming Herndon recorded their statements accurately, there is no hearsay in their testimony, only aging and potentially faulty memories.

(*Left*) Mentor Graham. Library of Congress. (*Right*) McGrady Rutledge. Mentor Graham and McGrady Rutledge both are said to have claimed they were told directly by Lincoln and Ann Rutledge of their love affair. Library of Congress.

In a letter to Herndon dated April 2, 1866, Mentor Graham, New Salem's schoolteacher, wrote, "Lincoln and she was Engaged—*Lincoln told me so—she intimated to me the same*" (emphasis added).[24] McGrady Rutledge's testimony, on the other hand, comes indirectly from Robert Rutledge, who wrote to Herndon on November 21, 1866: "Mr. Lincoln, Courted Ann and engaged to marry her, on the completion of the study of law. In this I am corroborated by James [McGrady] Rutledge a cousin about her age & who was in her confidence, he say in a letter to me just received, 'Ann told me once in coming from a Camp Meeting on Rock creek, that engagements made too far a hed sometimes failed, that one had failed [meaning her engagement with Mc-Namar] *Ann gave me to understand, that as soon as certain studies were completed she and Lincoln would be married*" (emphasis added).[25]

The third witness, Isaac Cogdal, was a former resident of New

Salem overlapping Lincoln's stay there in the early years. At Lincoln's urging, Cogdal studied for the law and became a lawyer in Illinois in 1860. Cogdal is historian John Y. Simon's linchpin for accepting the Lincoln–Ann Rutledge romance. The importance of Cogdal as a witness lies in the fact that his testimony discusses his visit with Lincoln in 1860, just six years prior to Herndon's letter of inquiry. Such a visit would be presumably still fresh in Cogdal's memory. In his letter to Herndon, Cogdal wrote an interesting narrative quoting Lincoln:

> He [Lincoln] became acquainted with Miss Ann Rutledge in 1831—2 & 3. He courted her—and after he was elected presdt. He said to me one day—"Ike call at my office in the State house about an hour by sun down. The Company will then all be gone. I want to enquire about old times and old acquaintances" Said Lincoln. He then said—"When we lived in Salem there were the Greens, Potters Armstrongs—& Rutledges. These folks have got scattered all over the world—some are dead—where are the Rutledges—Greens—&c." "After we had spoken over old times —persons—circumstances—in which he showed wonderful memory I then dared to ask him this question—May I now in turn ask you one question Lincoln, said Cogdal Most assuredly. "I will answer your question if a fair one with all my heart"— then it was that he answered—as follows "Abe is it true that you fell in love with & courted Ann Rutledge," said Cogdal. Lincoln said, "it is true—true indeed I did. I have loved the name of Rutledge to this day. I have kept my mind on their movements ever since & love them dearly"—said Lincoln. Abe—is it true—said Cogdal, that you ran a little wild about the matter: "I did really —I ran off the track: It was my first. I loved the woman dearly & sacredly: she was a handsome girl—would have made a good loving wife—was natural & quite intellectual, though not highly Educated—I did honestly—& truly love the girl & think often —often of her now."[26]

Historians James G. Randall and Charles A. Tripp attack the statement contextually for its "unLincolnian quality," stating that "hardly a phrase of it could pass as likely Lincoln language."[27] Randall's and Tripp's first criticism centers on Lincoln's nature never to discuss private matters. Lincoln was a private person, obsessively so. There is no evidence of Lincoln ever discussing such private or intimate matters as his love life with anyone. Still, that cannot serve as the sole basis for rejecting Cogdal. Modern technology, especially computers, allows analyses in ways never done before. The way one writes is often as distinctive as one's fingerprints. Each of us has a pattern akin to literary DNA, and given the right expert using the proper technology it is possible to read one's literary DNA. Tripp conducts just such an analysis of Cogdal's quotations of Lincoln: "if Lincoln had chosen to answer such a question at all [regarding his love for Ann Rutledge], nothing in his style suggests that he would have stammered it out three or four times in one phrase after the other, with the likes of, 'It is true— true indeed,' or that he 'did honestly & truly love the girl,' or that he thinks 'often—often of her now.'"[28] Other examples from Cogdal's statement include "dearly & sacredly," and "honestly and truly." Of course, it is Cogdal attempting to quote Lincoln, not Lincoln himself speaking. In the end, Tripp agrees with Randall in dismissing Cogdal's statement, rather harshly writing, "his entire testimony reeks of *deliberate fraud*," comparing it to "Piltdown Man and crop circles."[29]

The naysayers of Lincoln's love affair with Ann Rutledge disregard the multitude of Herndon's informants, agreeing with James G. Randall that such recollections are too "dim and misty" to be taken seriously. While thousands of words have been written refuting these witnesses, their rejection still comes down to "dim and misty." Memories cannot be trusted, especially after thirty years.

It is true that inconsistencies exist among the two dozen informants claiming a love affair and engagement existed, but these differences are minor and do not negate the underlying claim that Lincoln and Ann were in love and engaged to be married. To reject this claim one has to believe all two dozen lied, or independently were influenced by some outside entity, such as Herndon, to believe such a relationship existed, or that Herndon falsified his record. If two or three people were the basis for the story, it is certainly plausible they lied, were mistaken, or were coached into believing a relationship existed. But discarding the word of two dozen informants would require an adept deconstruction of their testimony. While much of the testimony is classified as hearsay (person one was told by person two, etc.), there are the three informants who claim to have heard from either Ann Rutledge or Lincoln or both directly. They cannot be dismissed as hearsay.

Isaac Cogdal is one such informant. The naysayers have disregarded his testimony as "deliberate fraud" based on his ascribing unbelievable language to Lincoln. But even if Cogdal misquoted or even reconstructed Lincoln's language, paraphrasing what he believed Lincoln said, one must conclude he was a deliberate liar. The objection of "dim and misty" memory does not apply to Cogdal since he made his statement only six years after he claimed to have heard it, not thirty.

What of Mentor Graham and McGrady Rutledge? Both men were considered honorable. Graham said, "Lincoln and she was engaged—*Lincoln told me so—she intimated to me the same* [emphasis added]." McGrady said, "Ann gave me to understand, that as soon as certain studies were completed she and Lincoln would be married."[30] We would have to convict both men of the same crime as Cogdal, "deliberate fraud."

The yea-sayers believe that to indict all of Herndon's informants with faulty memories or deliberate lying is unrealistic. After all, reminiscences and recollections are the stock and trade of most historians. Where would we be if we refused to use the memories of people of events in the past? This is especially true for Lincoln studies, where historians rely heavily on the reminiscences of such people as Ward Hill Lamon, John Hay, John George Nicolay, Dennis Hanks, and Sarah Bush Johnston Lincoln to name just a few. Too often, it seems, we pick and choose our sources when it suits us.[31]

The thorough historian, however, requires corroboration of any recollection, and often more than one corroborator; three is always better than two. In the case of Ann Rutledge and Lincoln we have two dozen, and while they may differ in small details they all seem to agree that a romantic attraction existed, and some agree that an engagement took place.

But what about John McNamar? While he was not present in New Salem during the period when the affair began and flourished, he certainly should have heard something about his fiancée having an affair with his good friend Lincoln during his absence. McNamar arrived back in New Salem two weeks after Ann's death. He put a marker on her grave. In a letter to Herndon's father-in-law (who was corresponding with McNamar on Herndon's behalf), McNamar wrote, "Mr. Lincoln was not to my knowledge paying any particular attention to any of the young ladies of my acquaintance when I left— there was no rivalry between him and myself on that score." That would seem obvious. Later in the same letter he wrote, "I never heard any person say that Mr. Lincoln addressed Miss Ann Rutledge in terms of courtship neither her own family nor my acquaintances otherwise. I heard simply this expression from two prominent Gentlemen of my acquaintance and Personal Friends that Lincoln was Grieved very much at her death."[32]

In a later letter dated December 1, 1866, McNamar writes that he thought Lincoln's deep depression was related to "a lovers disappointment with regard to the Lady whom he afterwards married."[33] McNamar is referring to Mary Todd, not Ann Rutledge, and an event that took place in 1841, not 1835.

The statements by McNamar would support the naysayers, who do not believe a romance existed. However, it is not unreasonable to believe that no one would tell McNamar that his fiancée went behind his back and had a romantic affair with his friend Lincoln. While McNamar's understanding is interesting, it is not definitive.

There are two other individuals we need to add to our story, Matthew Marsh and Mary Owens. Marsh, a New Salem resident and friend of Lincoln, wrote a letter to his brother, George M. Marsh, twenty-two days after Ann Rutledge's death. In his letter, Marsh writes: "The Post Master (Mr. Lincoln), is very careless about leaving his office open and unlocked during the day—half the time I go in and get my papers, etc., without anyone being there as was the case yesterday [September 21]. The letter was only marked twenty-five and even if he had been there and known it was double, he would not have charged me any more—luckily he is a very clever fellow and a particular friend of mine. If he is there when I carry this to the office—I will get him to Frank it."[34] It turns out Lincoln was there and did "frank" the envelope, writing, "Free, A. Lincoln, P.M. New Salem, Ill. Sept. 22." This letter and Lincoln's use of his free franking privileges three weeks after Ann Rutledge's death is cited by the naysayers as proof that Lincoln did not suffer for weeks from a "suicidal depression." It is used by the yea-sayers as proof that Lincoln suffered some sort of breakdown. They point to his absence from his duties, leaving his post office unattended, and violating postal law by free franking an envelope of a friend as proof of his severe depression. The naysayers reinforce their argument by pointing out that a few days after the letter incident Lincoln conducted a survey of a piece of farmland for Marsh. The survey required skill and an attention to detail not expected of someone in the deep throes of depression and unable to function. As with most controversies surrounding Lincoln, the same set of facts are used to support opposing views—reminiscent of the young boy who got his facts right, but got his conclusions wrong.

That Lincoln showed signs of grief seems clear. At least every-

Site of the cabin where Ann Rutledge died on August 25, 1835. Photograph by Edward Steers Jr.

one agrees Lincoln "ran off the rails." The question is why and for how long. The "free franking" incident and farm survey suggest that if Lincoln was seriously depressed at Ann's death, he recovered within a few weeks and returned to his normal self.

Lincoln had experienced grief on numerous occasions, beginning with the death of his mother when a boy of nine, and his older sister, Sarah, when he was nineteen. Lincoln is generally described as a sad, melancholy man. Could his grief at Ann's death be that of a close friend who had difficulty seeing so young a person die from a terrible disease, and not the result of a love affair? Or could Lincoln have been in love with Ann without her reciprocating? More importantly, if Ann Rutledge was Lincoln's true love, she was not his only one. During the period of Lincoln's alleged courtship of Ann Rutledge, the sister of one of New Salem's more prosperous residents, Elizabeth Abell, visited New Salem in the fall of 1833. Lincoln was a

Mary Owens. Library of Congress.

close friend of Elizabeth and Bennett Abell. Elizabeth Abell's sister, Mary Owens, came to New Salem to visit with her after John Mc-Namar had been absent for nearly a year and after the Rutledge family, including Ann, had moved seven miles north of New Salem to Sandridge. According to several of Herndon's informants, Lincoln visited the Abells on numerous occasions during Mary Owens's stay, and the two became close friends. The friendship blossomed into much more, and an understanding of marriage soon developed.

Mary Owens returned to her Kentucky home after several months of visiting her sister. In the fall of 1836, about twelve months after Ann Rutledge's death, she returned to New Salem. Lincoln, having previously suggested marriage, began to have doubts. Lincoln now saw Mary in a different light. She was much heavier and older than he remembered from her first visit. His feeling of obligation to honor his agreement to marry Mary left him in a quandary. During Mary's second stay in New Salem, Lincoln obtained his law license and moved to Springfield to join the law firm of his mentor, John T. Stuart.

That the obligation of marriage to Mary was real and weighed heavily on Lincoln's mind is obvious from two letters he wrote to Mary from Springfield. Lincoln's letters were filled with doubt and equivocation. Lincoln wrote, "You would have to be poor without the means of hiding your poverty." And, "What you have said to me [about marriage] may have been in jest, or I may have misunderstood it. If so, then let it be forgotten." He closed his first letter writing, "What I have said I will most positively abide by, *provided you wish it*" (emphasis added).[35] In his second letter to Mary he was more to the point, "I now say that you can now drop the subject [marriage], dismiss your thoughts (if you ever had any) from me forever, and leave this letter unanswered, without calling forth one accusing murmur from me."[36]

The relationship, including the proposal of marriage, ended. In a letter to William Herndon in May 1866, Mary Owens wrote, "Mr. Lincoln was deficient in those little links which make up the great chain of a woman's happiness."[37] Clearly, Mary took Lincoln up on his offer to "drop the subject."

The affair between Lincoln and Mary Owens that led to an engagement twelve months after Ann's death certainly dismisses the claim by Herndon that Lincoln would never love another woman again. If Lincoln's heart was buried in Ann's grave, it did not take long to resurrect it.

There is one last point to be made on the question of a love affair. The naysayers rightly point out that all of the informants were queried after Ann and Lincoln were dead, and that Herndon queried them in such a way as to lead them in their testimony. This is a valid criticism. Informants may well have been influenced by Herndon, and by one another, biasing their answers. At this point we need to hear from one last informant, John Hill.

John Hill (1839–1898) was the son of New Salem's Samuel Hill and Parthena Nance Hill. Parthena is one of Herndon's twenty-four informants (Sam Hill is not, having died in 1857), although her testimony comes through a second person, thus falling under hearsay. John Hill was born in New Salem in 1839, when the village was in its death throes. That was four years after Ann Rutledge's death and two years after Lincoln moved to Springfield. As such, he had no first-hand knowledge of the alleged romance. Here the story becomes interesting. Shortly after his birth, he and his parents moved to Petersburg, two miles north of New Salem. In adult life, Hill became editor of the Democratic Petersburg newspaper, the *Menard Axis.* An opponent of Lincoln, Hill supported Stephen Douglas in the 1858 senatorial race and again in the 1860 presidential race. In 1862, while Lincoln was in the White House, and *three years before Herndon began his research* into Lincoln's early life, Hill wrote an article that appeared in the *Menard Axis* under the title "A Romance of Reality." An excerpt from the article appearing in the February 15, 1862, issue stated:

He [Lincoln] now became an actor in a new scene. He chanced to meet with a lady, who to him seemed lovely, angelic, and the height of perfection. Forgetful of all things else, he could think or dream of naught but her. His feelings he soon made her acquainted with, and was delighted with reciprocation. This to him was perfect happiness and with uneasy anxiety he awaited the arrival of the day when the twin would be made one flesh.— But that day was doomed never to arrive. Disease came upon this lovely beauty, and she sickened and died. The youth had wrapped his heart with hers, and this was more than he could bear. He saw her to her grave, and as the cold clods fell upon the coffin, he sincerely wished that he too had been enclosed within it. Melancholy came upon him; he was changed and sad. His friends detected strange conduct and a flighty imagination—

They placed him under guard for fear of his committing sui-
cide.—New circumstances changed his thoughts, and at length
he partially forgot that which had for a time consumed his
mind.[38]

This is a definitive piece of evidence in our story. Lincoln was alive at
the time and located in the White House. Herndon was in Springfield
practicing law and unaware of Ann Rutledge or a romance. Lincoln
was well aware of John Hill, as evidenced by a lengthy response by
Lincoln to a pamphlet published by Hill during the presidential campaign of 1860. Hill attacked Lincoln on his position of abolishing slavery in the District of Columbia. Lincoln's lengthy response takes Hill
to task for deliberately misrepresenting his position. The response is
written as if by a person other then Lincoln, and appears to never
have been sent to Hill for publication.[39]

 While Lincoln knew of John Hill, and read his writings during
the 1860 campaign, there is no evidence that he was aware of the Hill
article or its contents at the time of its publication in 1862. If he was,
he left no comment. It refutes, however, any belief that Herndon
played a role in creating the story of a Lincoln-Rutledge romance, for
all indication is that Herndon knew nothing about the Hill article
and learned of it only when John Hill responded to Herndon's general inquiry in June 1865, after Herndon had already learned of the alleged romance from his other informants.[40]

 The story of a romance predates Herndon and his informants.
This means that to discredit the story one must discredit John Hill
or his source, not Herndon. Interestingly, Roy P. Basler, editor of *The
Collected Works of Abraham Lincoln*, in an annotated footnote, points
out that Lincoln's claim that Hill lacked "respect for truth" gives cre-
dence to the belief that he made up the story of a Lincoln–Ann Rutledge romance.[41] Basler does point out that Hill, and not Herndon,
deserves credit for first publishing the story of a romance.

 Why would Hill make up such a story? Hill's source, presumably, was his mother (and/or father). John's mother wrote to Herndon in 1887, two years before Herndon and Weik's biography of Lincoln appeared, and long after Herndon had initiated his research. In her letter Parthena Hill wrote, "Lincoln took advantage of McNamar's absence—Courted Ann—got her confidence &c and were in Mr [Sam] Hills & my opinion—as well as the opinion of others that they were engaged." Later in the letter she wrote, "I think that if McNamar had got back from NY before Ann's death that she would have married McNamar."[42] This latter statement is used by the naysayers to throw the alleged relationship into question. The letter, of course, is written years after Herndon first gave his lecture and knowledge of an alleged affair was widespread. Samuel Hill's testimony is strictly hearsay, appearing in his wife's letter. He had been dead for thirty years. Parthena Hill's letter strongly suggests that John Hill learned of the romantic affair in 1862 from his mother.

Whatever the source, John Hill's article is the strongest evidence of a romantic affair and engagement between Ann Rutledge and Lincoln. It stands alone among all of the yea-sayers. In 1944, Lincoln historian and bibliographer Jay Monaghan published an account of the Hill article in the *Abraham Lincoln Quarterly* under the title "New Light on the Lincoln-Rutledge Romance." In his concluding remarks Monaghan writes, "Certainly future Lincoln biographers will have to reckon with John Hill's account. They can no longer dismiss the story as a figment of an unhappy Herndon's frustrated mind."[43]

The eminent historian James G. Randall, who is credited with destroying the story of a Lincoln-Rutledge romance, does discuss the Hill article. While acknowledging the article in his dismissal of the story because it "has a certain priority in that it is pre-Herndonian," he nevertheless dismisses it, stating it had flaws in describing Lincoln as a person, and Hill's "memories were indirect [through his father]."[44] That is all Randall writes. There is no further analysis.

This hardly discredits the article. While Hill's account is hearsay, it is no less a source than many of the sources Randall uses in his excellent four-volume biography of Lincoln. Too many Lincoln authors give hearsay a bad name yet use hearsay often enough in their own works, as does Randall.

As stated at the beginning of this chapter, historians are divided over the authenticity of the Lincoln-Rutledge romance. It would appear that nothing short of discovering a letter between the two Salemites expressing their love for one another would change anyone's opinion. What makes this story so fascinating is that historians treasure truth. It is their stock in trade. Any historian worth his or her salt works diligently to discover the truth about their subject. The Lincoln-Rutledge romance is one of those areas of history where numerous historians have spent untold time digging for the truth with differing results. We all have the same facts; it is our conclusions that differ, which makes history all the more interesting. Historian Richard Nelson Current perhaps stated it best when he wrote, "This much is believable, *though not proven*: Abraham Lincoln was once in love with Ann" (emphasis added).[45] John Hill's 1862 article supports Current's conclusion.

Proof from beyond the Grave

Yours Affectionately, Abe

In chapter 3 we were left with the conclusion that only a letter between Lincoln and Ann Rutledge acknowledging a love affair and engagement would satisfy the skeptics—not an unreasonable demand. Nearly a century later such a letter surfaced; in fact, several letters surfaced. The alleged romance between Abraham Lincoln and Ann Rutledge is the gift that keeps on giving. The real gift turned out to be several letters between the two star-crossed lovers that came to light when a young woman from San Diego, California, contacted the editor of the *Atlantic Monthly*'s book division, Edward A. Weeks, in June 1928. Wilma Frances Minor, a young would-be author, had written "the true love story" of Abraham Lincoln and Ann Rutledge based on a collection of letters and related manuscript materials that descended through her mother's family.[1] It was a veritable treasure trove of documents. Among the materials in the collection were several letters between the young Lincoln and Ann Rutledge that told of their love for one another and their plans to marry. It was a godsend to those who believed a love affair existed between the two New Salemites.

The story of Abraham Lincoln's love for the beautiful Ann Rutledge warmed the hearts of most romantics. It was in the pioneer village of New Salem in the 1830s that the two lovers met and fell in love. The poet-biographer Carl Sandburg gave renewed life to the legend. "The pink-fair face, and mouth and eyes in a frame of light corn-silk hair" caused Lincoln to tremble when "she spoke so simple a

Wilma Frances Minor.
Fehrenbacher lecture pamphlet
published by the Louis A.
Warren Library and Museum.

thing as, 'the corn is getting high, isn't it?'" It was Sandburg who
more than anyone gave life to the romantic story. Most historians
were skeptical, but now, at long last, was proof.

Minor had written an article based on the manuscript materials passed down through generations, and she wanted to enter it in
the magazine's annual nonfiction book award contest. The winning
author would receive $5,000, a considerable sum in 1928, and publi-
cation of an article in the prestigious magazine. It was a young author's dream.

Weeks was stunned by the writer's claim of an unknown cache
of Lincoln material. He took Minor's letter to the *Atlantic*'s editor,

Ellery Sedgwick, who was skeptical of such an important find. In his memoir published years later, Weeks wrote, "One could not shut out the possibility of what the letters would mean to the magazine and the Atlantic Press if they could be proved genuine."[2]

Sedgwick wrote to Minor asking her to send photostatic copies of the documents. Minor complied. In all, there were fourteen letters, ten written by Lincoln and four by Ann Rutledge. The entire collection included several pages from the diary of Ann's cousin, Matilda Cameron, a "memorandum" written by Sally Calhoun (daughter of John Calhoun, the county surveyor who hired Lincoln in New Salem as his deputy), four books with Lincoln's signature, and various annotations by Lincoln. It was an incredible collection of material far surpassing any known archive of the village of New Salem.

Impressed with the materials, Sedgwick arranged for Minor to visit the *Atlantic* offices in person. Whatever doubts Sedgwick and Weeks had were soon dispelled during their first meeting. Wilma, Weeks wrote, was "a handsome woman with a curvaceous figure, seductive grey-blue eyes, and a charming manner."[3] Sedgwick, in particular, was smitten. A deal was struck, and Wilma was given a contract to write her book based on the manuscripts. Sedgwick gave her a $1,000 advance and a guarantee of $4,000 on publication. In the meantime, Wilma would write three articles to be published in the *Atlantic* based on her collection.

Although convinced of the letters' authenticity, Sedgwick was careful enough to submit them to several well-known Lincoln authorities for their approval. His first choice was the eminent Lincoln author and first-rate researcher William E. Barton. Barton had just recently published two books on Lincoln based on extensive research into numerous primary records.[4] No one could challenge his position as a Lincoln scholar.

Invited to the offices of the *Atlantic,* Barton viewed the photo-

Ida Minerva Tarbell. Library of Congress.

static copies Wilma had sent Sedgwick. Barton was concerned that both the number and the content of the material were unusually large. Such a discovery was unique among Lincoln material, and Barton should know, having researched Lincoln for over twenty years. If authentic, Wilma's collection would be the greatest discovery of Lincoln documents ever.

Despite his initial skepticism, Barton concluded the documents were real. They were, he said, "remarkably consistent and satisfactory."[5] The documents were unquestionably real. Enthused, Sedgwick next turned to Ida Tarbell, the "muckraking" investigative journalist who authored a four-volume biography on Lincoln.[6] Tarbell had been fascinated with Lincoln ever since she was a young girl.

By the time Tarbell arrived at the *Atlantic* offices, Wilma had turned over the original documents to Sedgwick. Tarbell examined them carefully—like Barton, she was skeptical at so important a find. In the end, the investigative journalist gave her blessing, stating, "My faith is strong that you have an amazing set of true Lincoln documents."[7]

Although convinced of the documents' authenticity, Sedgwick pressed on, seeking further validation. Next on his list of experts was Worthington Chauncey Ford, former head of the Manuscript Division of the Library of Congress and currently the editor of the Massachusetts Historical Society publications. Ford examined the same material as Barton and Tarbell and pronounced the letters by Lincoln as forgeries. They bore no resemblance to Lincoln's handwriting, he said, even as early as 1834. Lincoln, Ford proclaimed, did not write the letters.

Sedgwick was shaken by Ford's positive claim of forgery but soon concluded that Ford was jealous that he had not been the first asked to examine the letters. Sedgwick decided to call on one more Lincoln historian to shore up the documents' authenticity, Carl Sandburg. Sandburg looked over the material and was thrilled. "These new letters seem entirely authentic, and preciously and wonderfully co-ordinate and chime with all else known of Lincoln. Students of Lincoln's personal development will prize and love them for several known reasons, and for intangible and inexplicable reasons."[8]

Sedgwick completed his investigation by calling on a forensic chemist to examine the paper and ink. Such analyses are objective, unlike the views of experts evaluating content. The paper and ink proved consistent with the documents' supposed age. The only analysis left was the handwriting, and since no known examples by Rutledge, Cameron, or Calhoun existed, it left only Lincoln's writing available, which had already passed the scholarly eyes of Barton, Tarbell, and Sandburg, but not Ford. To top matters off, Herbert Putnam, the Librarian of Congress, wanted to display the documents at his prestigious library following publication in the *Atlantic*.

The legend of a Lincoln-Rutledge romance had become imprinted in the minds of the general public through the writing of Carl Sandburg in the first of his two-volume set, *Abraham Lincoln: The Prairie Years*, which covered Lincoln's early years. His beautiful prose captured the public's imagination, and the initial sales topped a half million copies.[9] It is a love story that simply will not die.

While Sandburg's version of the Lincoln-Rutledge romance became part of American folklore, it was rejected by the country's leading historians as more fiction than fact. To historians such as James G. Randall and Allan Nevins, the evidence did not rise to a standard high enough to be believable. Now, at last, was proof that a romance not only existed, but also was destined to end in marriage. The Lincoln historical community was turned on its ear. Randall and Nevins would have to eat crow.

The December issue of the *Atlantic Monthly* magazine published the first of its three articles under the provocative title "Lincoln the Lover." It included excerpts from Minor's newly discovered letters between the two lovers. The article began by boldly pointing out that many historians denied such a relationship existed. The story was a myth created by Lincoln's close friend and law partner, William Herndon, in his infamous Springfield lecture, "Lincoln and Ann Rutledge and the Pioneers of New Salem."[10] The Minor documents put the debate to rest once and for all; Abe loved Ann, and she loved him. Wilma wrote in her first article, "Now it becomes possible to reveal in full light and at first hand the story, so full of tenderness and hope, so tragic in its close, which has hitherto rested on contestable report. Not only did Lincoln and Ann hold each other dear; the actual letters which passed between them remain."[11]

Wilma's first article contained two letters from Lincoln to John Calhoun, Lincoln's surveyor friend who hired Lincoln as his assistant. In addition, there were three excerpts from Sally Calhoun's diary in which she writes, "Father predicts great things in the future for Lincoln, for he says Lincoln has character."[12] In her second article, titled "The Courtship," Minor draws from the diary of Matilda "Mat" Cameron, Ann Rutledge's cousin. Mat writes, "I am so happy coz now that Abe Lincoln and my deerest friend Ann are a ingaged cupel . . ." and further, "Abe and Ann are awful in love he rites her leters."[13]

It is not until eight pages into the second of the three articles that we finally hear from "Abe." In 1833, Ann's father moved the entire family seven miles north of New Salem to the small community of Sandridge. Apparently this move so distanced the two lovers that they communicated by mail. In one letter, Lincoln writes, "My beloved Ann, I am happy to ask you to accompany me to literary they have planned for you to sing and I am to recite. I could write to you forever but Nance will not wait that long. With great affection, Abe."[14]

After moving to Sandridge, James Rutledge's loss of steady income forced Ann and her sisters to hire out as housekeepers. Ann worked for Lincoln's good friend "Uncle" Jimmy Short, who lived a short distance from the Rutledge house. Lincoln, lamenting Ann's situation having to work as a scour maid, writes:

My beloved Ann; I am filled with regret over the defect of the conduct of a fate that has bourne down so heavily upon you and yours. I try to persuade myself that my unlucky star has not overshadowed you. Molly Prewitt told me about you going to work for James Short family, you are too frail for that hard work. My treasured one I should now be standing between you and such trials. O! When will success crown my untiring efforts. I sicken at many failures especially as no more am I lazy in the discharge of my duties. Forgive this long-faced letter, as I now should be upholding you in hope for the future, for I but today have been greatly assured of my election as member to the Legislature. So perhaps our dreams will come true. I am borrowing Jack's horse to ride over to see you this coming Saturday. Cutting my foot prevents my walking. I will be at your pleasure to accompany you to the Sand Ridge taffy-pull. I will be glad to hear your good Father's sermon on the Sabbath. I feel unusually lifted with hope of relieving your present worry at an early date and likewise doing myself the best turn of my life. With you my beloved all things are possible. Now James kindly promises to deliver into your dear little hands this letter. May the good Lord speed Saturday afternoon.

Affectionately A. Lincoln

The third installment came in the February 1929 issue. Titled "The Tragedy," it began in 1834 with Lincoln's third year in New Salem and Ann's second year at Sandridge. Ann gives Lincoln her mother's Bible, writing, "I love it so much that I want you to hav it. Ples read it all. It will make you feel different."[15] Lincoln accepts the Bible and annotates portions of it, writing in part, "I will be diligent in my reading. A. Lincoln."[16]

The article also contains additional excerpts from "Mat" Cameron's diary and Ann's last letter to her "Beloved Abe." Ann has fallen ill with a "cole," and writes Lincoln not to "cum to-nite," but "to cum tomoro nite eny-way."[17] Lincoln writes back, "My Dearly Valued Ann, I have been saying over and over to myself surely my traditional bad luck cannot reach me again through my beloved. I do long to confirm the confidence you have in heaven—but should anything serious occur to you I fear my faith would be eternally broken. My fervent love is with you. Yours affectionately Abe."[18]

Ann's "cole" soon develops into "brain fever," or more likely typhoid fever, and after a few days lingering between life and death Lincoln is sent for to come see her. Ann dies on August 25, 1835. With Ann's death Lincoln falls into a deep depression. There were tales of his visiting Ann's gravesite and throwing himself on her grave to protect her from the harsh rain and driving snowstorms. His friends feared for his life.[19]

Despite his deep despair and strange behavior, Lincoln had enough presence of mind to give Ann's love letters to her cousin Mat Cameron for safekeeping. Mat recorded the events in her diary, "The kin ses Abe is luny. I think he is braken-harted. He wants me to keep his 5 letters from her coz he is perswaded he will sune foler her I expect he will."[20]

And so the beautiful love story between Ann and Abe comes to a tragic end. The controversial love affair was confirmed at long last thanks to the precious collection of letters and documents brought to light by Wilma Frances Minor, and published for all to read by Ellery Sedgwick and the *Atlantic Monthly*. The tragic love story warmed the hearts of the American public until the fourth installment appeared in the April 1929 issue. The article was written by a young and able Lincoln scholar new to the field named Paul Angle. Angle, through his exceptional scholarship, exposed the entire collection as a fabrication and Wilma Frances Minor as a fraud. Angle's analysis began to turn the previous support of William Barton and Carl Sandburg, raising doubts in their minds. In the beginning, only Worthington Chauncey Ford had dismissed the collection as a fabrication. Now Angle had proven it, and Ellery Sedgwick, to his credit, agreed to allow Angle to publish his devastating rebuke in the *Atlantic Monthly*.

Handwriting and literary analysis are valuable tools in examining any document, but they are entirely subjective tools. The history of literature is replete with documents authenticated by experts only later proven to be fabricated. The Mormon documents and Oath of a Freeman, the Tartar Rebellion Map, dozens of Lincoln letters, papyrus containing references to Jesus's wife, the Hitler Diaries, a poem by Emily Dickinson, all authenticated only to be proven false. Authentication requires more than subjective analysis. It requires authentication of internal evidence. Fabricators have a habit of too often making mistakes of fact that eventually trip them up when scrutinized by scholars. Forensic evidence can be faked. Aged paper, formulated ink, recreated type—all have been tried, with occasional success. But mistakes of fact in the body of documents often prove the best test of all. In the missing pages from John Wilkes Booth's diary, the writer has Booth referring to his own brother by the wrong name, an alleged letter by Lincoln places him in the wrong place on the wrong date, a diary entry refers to the woman's husband as dead when he is alive and well, and on and on. Such is the case with Paul Angle's analysis of the Minor collection.

What may be the most egregious error Angle discovered is the comment by Ann Rutledge in one of her "Abe letters" in which she writes, "I am gratefull for the Spencers copy-book I copy frum that every time I can spair." Ann died in 1835, but *Spencer's Copybook* was not published until 1848, thirteen years after her death.

Angle next analyzes a letter from Lincoln to John Calhoun, the man who hired Lincoln as his deputy surveyor. Lincoln writes: "Dear friend John if you have in your possession or can tell me where you left the Certificate of Survey of Joshua Blackburn's Claim there seems some controversy between him and Green concerning that North Section 40." Section 40? No such designation exists in surveying. Townships were laid out as a square, six miles by six miles, with each section being one square mile. Thus, there were only thirty-six sections to a survey—no section forty.[21]

Angle's most devastating find concerned Mat Cameron and her illuminating diary. According to Angle, Mat Cameron did not exist. She was a made-up character meant to embellish the letters. To make matters worse for Wilma Minor, neither did Sally Calhoun. Angle could find no contemporary records of either woman, including in family Bibles and numerous documents. While negative proof—the absence of finding these two women—is not conclusive, Angle went on to show that several of Mat Cameron's diary entries mention Martha Calhoun, a dear friend, who was not born until 1843, ten years after she appears in Mat Cameron's diary.

Angle's extensive analysis of the documents leaves no doubt as to their fabrication. While the fabricator was knowledgeable about many aspects of New Salem, and of Abe and Ann, she was not familiar enough to avoid such glaring errors.

Sedgwick, of course, confronted Wilma only to learn that she originally approached the publisher of the *San Diego Union* newspaper with her material. She had been hired to write a weekly column titled "Sidelights on Life." Among those she interviewed for her column was Scott Greene, the son of Billy Greene of New Salem, Lincoln's store partner. At this time, Wilma told her editor that Scott Greene had a large collection of materials from New Salem including love letters between Lincoln and Ann Rutledge. Wilma convinced Greene to sell her the collection. The documents, it turns out, had not descended in her family as she had told Sedgwick.

Sedgwick next hired a detective to visit Wilma and her mother in San Diego and find out what really went on regarding the collection. When confronted with the evidence, the two women first blamed Billy Greene's son Scott. It was Scott who had put one over on Wilma and her mother. The two women held to their story.

Sedgwick, still under Wilma's spell, decided to attack Paul Angle, publishing a copy of a letter Angle wrote to his parents boasting of his success in exposing the fabrication: "It's the biggest thing that ever happened to me. One doesn't very often get a chance to put the magazine of the country [the *Atlantic Monthly*] in the frying pan and cook it brown."[22] Even so, Angle's criticism and evidence held up despite Sedgwick's efforts to embarrass him.

Sedgwick sent one of his better staff members, Teresa Fitzpatrick, to interview Wilma and press her on just where the documents came from, and the true story behind them. Wilma finally confessed. Wilma told Fitzpatrick that after interviewing Scott Greene a light bulb went off in her head. She went to her mother, who was a professional psychic. The two women concocted an even more fantastic story. Wilma's mother set about contacting the people of New Salem, including Lincoln and Rutledge, through Wilma's dead uncle in a seance. It seems Wilma's mother was in regular contact with the dead uncle. Wilma would have her mother ask the uncle specific questions about Lincoln and Rutledge. The uncle would then go and speak with the long deceased people and ask them Wilma's questions. In subsequent trances, the uncle would pass on the information he gleaned from his conversations with Lincoln and Ann Rutledge as well as Mat Cameron and Sally Calhoun. Wilma would then copy down the information, her hand guided by the spirits imitating their handwriting. The uncle even told Wilma where she could find old paper of the period in various endpapers of old books from the early 1800s.

You see, Wilma told Sedgwick, it was not a fraud because her mother actually had her dead uncle go and talk with the people getting the answers to her many questions. It was all true, having come from the spirits of the dead people. She and her mother were simply the recipients of the material. Sedgwick closed the case. He wanted no more to do with Wilma Frances Minor and her screwy mother. In journalistic fairness, Sedgwick granted Paul Angle permission to publish his own unedited article exposing the fraud. At the end of his article, Angle wrote, "To me, at least, a belief in the common authorship of these documents and the Gettysburg Address was impossible, and I much prefer the Gettysburg Address."[23]

To those of us who yearn for that piece of definitive proof of a Lincoln-Rutledge love affair, we will just have to wait for the next great discovery among long hidden documents. The good news: it is certain to happen again.

The modern tombstone over the alleged grave of Ann Rutledge in Oakland Cemetery, Petersburg, Illinois. The inscription on the stone is by Edgar Lee Masters from his book *Spoon River Anthology*. Photograph by Edward Steers Jr.

Little Crow, chief of the Dakota Sioux. National Portrait Gallery.

5

The Great White Father and the Dakota 38

While the President expressed no attitude toward the Indian other than to remember that one sneaked up behind his grandfather and killed him while he was working in a field, a double standard of race value might have had something to do with his treatment of the Sioux.

Lerone Bennett, *Forced into Glory*

The trials of the Dakota were conducted unfairly in a variety of ways. The evidence was sparse, the tribunal was biased, the defendants were unrepresented in unfamiliar proceedings conducted in a foreign language, and authority for convening the tribunal was lacking. More fundamentally, neither the Military Commission nor the reviewing authorities recognized that they were dealing with the aftermath of a war fought with a sovereign nation.

Carol Chomsky, University of Minnesota Law School

Redbud trees lined the banks of a meandering stream that gently flowed alongside the fertile bottomland of Kentucky soil. Known locally as "Long Run," it was less than two hundred yards from a stockade fort built as a refuge for the local settlers from marauding Indian attacks. The area had taken the ominous name of "Dark and Bloody Ground" from the various tribes' numerous battles. The sobriquet took on new meaning with the invasion of white settlers. Small raiding parties of young warriors roamed the area seeking to prove their bravery by taking white scalps. The year was 1786. It was a mild spring day, and the smell of freshly plowed earth filled the air. Captain Abraham Lincoln was busy sowing his summer crop. With him were his three young sons: Mordecai, the oldest, had just turned fifteen; Josiah was twelve, and Thomas, the youngest, was eight. Though young, all three boys worked hard at helping their father tend his fields.

Fighting Indians was not new to Captain Abraham Lincoln. Twice he joined the local militia from Rockingham County, Virginia, to secure the western border of the country's young frontier from attacking tribes. Lincoln had earned his title in 1774 in what was known as "Dunmore's War," and again during America's revolution in 1778. Receiving land warrants, in part for his militia service, Lincoln purchased two tracts of land in Virginia's westernmost county of Kentucky.[1] The commonwealth encouraged its residents to move west and settle the untamed region, expanding Virginia's land west of the Appalachian Mountains. It was in keeping with Lincoln's restless spirit, and he jumped at the opportunity.

Having moved his family to Kentucky in 1780, he once again faced the threat of hostile Indians. In Kentucky it became an occupational hazard. Indian raids were common, as small groups of roaming braves attacked vulnerable settlers whenever the opportunity arose.

It was while he was sowing his summer crop that two young Indians stealthily approached the father and his three boys, who were hard at work and oblivious to the impending danger. Their focus proved a fatal mistake. A single shot suddenly rang out, and a bullet pierced the veteran's chest, killing him instantly. The two Indians approached the lifeless body as the eldest son yelled to his middle brother to run to the nearby stockade fort for help. Eight-year-old Thomas sat by his father's lifeless body, crying. Mordecai quickly ran to the cabin, where he grabbed his father's rifle. Leveling it against the frame of the cabin door, he took aim at one of the Indians who approached young Thomas with his scalping knife glistening in the sun. The boy squeezed the trigger, setting off a brilliant flash followed by a loud explosion. The lead bullet found its mark, striking the Indian squarely in his chest, causing him to drop not ten feet from the crying Thomas. The second Indian, startled by the young boy's accuracy, turned and disappeared into the trees lining the bank of the stream.

Years later, Thomas Lincoln, a militiaman in his own right, told the story of his father's murder to his young son Abraham, named for his martyred grandfather. It made a deep impression on the boy. In 1859, in an autobiography written in preparation for a run at the Republican nomination for president, Lincoln wrote: "My paternal grandfather, Abraham Lincoln, emigrated from Rockingham County, Virginia, to Kentucky, about 1781 or 2 [the year was 1780], where, a year or two later, he was killed by Indians, not in battle, but by stealth, when he was laboring to open a farm in the forest."[2] It was a story that the young Abraham Lincoln would carry with him to his dying day.

Lincoln's interactions with Indians were a part of his adult life. As a young man living in the pioneer village of New Salem in 1832, like his grandfather and father before him, he answered the call of Illinois's governor, John Reynolds, for all patriotic men to defend their land against the "invading Indians" under the great Sauk chief, Black Hawk. Sixty-seven men from the surrounding area stepped forward, including the twenty-three-year-old Lincoln. To his everlasting pride, the men elected Lincoln their captain. In his autobiographical sketch written in 1859, Lincoln wrote, "I was elected a Captain of volunteers—a success which gave me more pleasure than any I have had since."[3]

Lincoln served three tours in the state militia, totaling ninety days of service. While he never saw action against Black Hawk and his warriors, Lincoln experienced every aspect of the campaign. He

The site of Captain Abraham Lincoln's cabin along Long Run. The old Long Run Baptist Church's stone foundation covers the original cabin site and grave of Abraham Lincoln's grandfather. Photograph by Edward Steers Jr.

A modern stone marker commemorates Lincoln's grandfather, killed by Indians in May 1786. Photograph by Edward Steers Jr.

faced a serious test of his leadership when an elderly Indian, named Potawatomi, wandered into his camp one evening. He carried a letter from the militia's commanding general stating that he was a friendly Indian who had often aided settlers. The note gave the old Indian safe passage among the white militia.

The note made no difference to the men who had enlisted to fight Indians. Several of them wanted to kill the old man. Lincoln stepped forward and said there would be no killing that evening. He told the men to respect the general's letter and welcome the Indian as a friend. When Lincoln's courage was challenged, he told the unruly men they would have to fight him first before killing the Indian. The men sullenly backed down and left the Indian in peace.[4]

Years later Abraham Lincoln had to deal with the Indian problem again, this time as president of the United States. As the Great White Father, it was his responsibility to oversee the care of the people who had killed his grandfather seventy-six years earlier. How he responded to this challenge is a story in itself.

On August 21, 1862, Secretary of War Edwin Stanton received a disturbing telegram from Alexander Ramsey, the governor of Minnesota: "The Sioux Indians on our western border have risen, and are murdering men, women, and children."[5] Ramsey's telegram gave no details. Within a matter of days, the Dakota Sioux Indians, under their chief, Little Crow, were marauding across a fifty-mile frontier, attacking and killing white settlers at an alarming rate. Ramsey, desperate for help in combating the uprising, contacted Lincoln and asked that the Civil War draft quota of fifty-two hundred men for Minnesota be postponed and that he send Union troops to help put down the uprising. The situation was becoming dire. Lincoln, struggling with a disastrous Civil War, was now forced to turn his attention to the Minnesota frontier.

Four years earlier, on May 11, 1858, Minnesota had become the thirty-second state. All along its western border was the federally

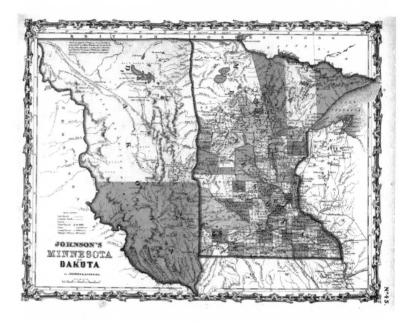

An 1860 map of Minnesota and the Dakota Territory. The uprising began in the southwestern region of the state. Wikimedia Commons.

established Dakota Territory.[6] In 1851, the Dakota Indians had signed a treaty with the federal government giving up 24 million acres of land within Minnesota in exchange for "annuities" paid in gold to the sum of $3 million. The annuities would allow the Dakotas to purchase all of their needs, such as food, clothing, and farming implements, and even to establish schools—all in exchange for their ancestral lands. They were left with a strip of land only ten miles wide and one hundred miles long along the Minnesota River. The Dakota people had to leave their ancestral land and exchange their traditional livelihood of independent living for one of dependence on federal annuities. The exchange might have worked had the federal government's Indian agents responsible for carrying out the terms of the treaty followed through with their end of the bargain.

The Indian agent system was infested with corruption, and it was the Indians who suffered. Of $96,000 allocated for payment to the Wahpekute and Mdewakanton bands (subtribes of the Dakota), only $800 was actually credited to these two Indian tribes.[7] Over $95,000 was falsely invoiced against the Indians, with agents pocketing the balance of the money. This scenario is trivial compared to the abuses and cheating that seemed endemic to the Indian agencies. People were hired for nonexistent jobs, invoices for farm implements were paid for nonexistent machinery, monthly annuities essential for purchasing food, blankets, clothing, and medical care were months in arrears. To top it off, settlers began to move onto Indian land in violation of treaties.

When the war came, it was not by plan, but by accident. It literally exploded into full-scale war with hundreds of deaths and dozens of atrocities of the most horrible kind. It all began on a lazy summer day in August 1862. Four young Dakota warriors had split off from a hunting party of twenty men. The men came upon a clutch of eggs located on the property of a white settler named Robinson Jones. One of the men took the eggs from the nest, only to be challenged by one of his companions. The eggs properly belonged to Jones, the Indian said, and if taken, might cause trouble. The men began to argue. At one point the word "coward" was used, daring the egg thief to kill a white man to prove his courage.

The four men then walked up to the farmhouse of Jones, where they found the farmer, his wife, two children, and a neighbor. The meeting began innocently, as Jones knew the Indians and had even lent one of his rifles to one of them. After a brief interlude in which Jones denied the Indians' request for food, he left and walked over to the home of his near neighbor, Howard Baker. The four Indians followed closely behind. As they talked, Jones reminded the Indian of the rifle and asked him to return it. The warrior denied ever having the gun. He then did a strange thing. He suggested the three of them have a shooting contest to see who was the best marksman. Jones and Baker agreed in an effort to placate the four Indians. It was at this point that one of the Indians suddenly turned his rifle on one of the men and shot him. Several other shots quickly followed, and all five of Baker's family were killed. It all happened within a minute for no apparent reason other than frustration and anger, which had been festering among the Indians.

The four Indians then returned to Jones's farm, where they stole two horses and galloped off, riding double. Returning to the Indian village at Rice Creek, they told their story to its chief, Red Middle Voice. He in turn went to the larger village headed by Chief Shakopee. After much discussion, they decided the seriousness of the killing required them to go to the chief of all the Dakotas, Little Crow. Considerable debate followed as to what action should be taken. The men argued over the question of war. The white men would seek retaliation for the killings. In the end, the advocates of war won out.

It was a moot point. By the morning after the incident at Baker's farm, word of the killings had spread and war exploded across the frontier. For fifty miles raiding parties of Dakota warriors swept through white settlements and agency compounds, burning and killing anything that moved. To many of the Indians, all of the enemy were considered combatants.

The morning following the initial killing at Baker's farm, a band of Dakota Indians attacked the Lower Sioux Agency, killing the agent and two of his employees. In the end, twenty people who had sought shelter at the agency were killed.[8] As the war progressed from days into weeks, "Entire families perished in their cabins or fields, or on the open roads attempting to flee. Dakota warriors took scores of women and children captive after killing the men."[9] No one was exempt from war.

As the war progressed, atrocities occurred with increasing frequency. Men were scalped and their bodies mutilated. Cabins were burned, "incinerating young children within."[10] One young woman, Justina Kriegert, recalled seeing a Dakota warrior "hack off the leg of her young niece,"[11] leaving her on the ground bleeding to death. In one of the most atrocious events, Caroline Waltz, several months pregnant, was cut open and "the child taken alive from the mother, and nailed to a tree."[12] Stories of finding babies and young children nailed to fences and doors abounded in the aftermath, but these stories were secondhand and related by people who were not eyewitnesses.

One eyewitness, however, was Mary Schwandt, an eighteen-year-old girl who lived with her family at Sacred Heart Creek. She was stopped by a marauding party of Indians while attempting to escape with three men and two young girls in a wagon. The three men were killed, and Schwandt and the two young girls were taken captive. They were then taken to a village where Schwandt was, "by force, taken to an unoccupied tepee near the house, and perpetrated the most horrible and nameless outrages on my person. These outrages were repeated at different times during my captivity."[13]

Eliza Swett in a letter to her sister Laura living in Clinton, Illinois, told of more atrocities, writing, "two children found alive nailed to the side of a house—others fastened to the ground by stakes driven through them. It is estimated that 200 women and children have been carried into captivity."[14] Through letters and newspaper articles, stories of such atrocities inflamed whites against the Dakota Sioux. Many of the Dakota Indians actually went out of their way—and at great personal risk to themselves—to rescue white settlers. Numerous stories were told of Indians warning settlers of marauding bands of warriors, sending them away from the Indians.

The actual number of dead is unknown, but estimates for the white settlers ranged from a low of eight hundred to a high of two thousand. There was no way to accurately determine the number killed. Bodies were scattered across the prairie only to decay or be

Refugees huddle together under the protection of Christian missionaries and friendly Indians. Photographer unknown, Wikimedia Commons.

eaten by animals. There are no estimates of Indian deaths, but the numbers were significantly lower than those of the white settlers, many of whom were defenseless.

Regardless of the actual numbers, it is certain that hundreds of people were killed, including Dakota Sioux. It is also true that atrocities were committed by Dakota warriors against women and children. On August 20, just three days after the first attack took place, Henry Hastings Sibley sent out word to all able-bodied men to take up arms and form a militia. Sibley, the first governor of Minnesota, was appointed by Governor Ramsey as colonel in charge of the state militia. Although Sibley was able to raise a fighting force, it was not enough to effectively combat the warring Dakota Sioux. Governor Ramsey appealed to President Lincoln to send troops to quell the uprising and restore peace.

Lincoln, engaged in his own war, was desperately in need of

Alexander Ramsey, governor of Minnesota at the time of the uprising. Library of Congress.

Major General John Pope. Following his defeat at the Second Battle of Bull Run, Lincoln sent Pope to Minnesota to put down the Dakota Sioux uprising. Library of Congress.

more troops to fill depleted ranks of Union regiments. He finally acquiesced to the frantic pleas of Governor Ramsey, ordering Major General John Pope and the 3rd, 4th, 9th, and 10th Regiments of the Minnesota Volunteer Infantry to Minnesota. Pope arrived in Minnesota on September 16, taking overall command of the fighting forces.

Pope had only recently commanded Union troops at the Second Battle of Bull Run, where Confederate general Robert E. Lee successfully defeated Union forces. Relieved of his command, Pope began haranguing Lincoln, claiming Major General Fitz John Porter was responsible for the disastrous defeat because he disobeyed Pope's orders. Porter was court-martialed and relieved of his command.[15]

Initially, Little Crow and his warriors scored several minor victories at Birch Coulee and Forest City, but Sibley's militia combined with the Minnesota troops was too great, and too well armed, eventually defeating Little Crow and his warriors. The final battle took place at Wood Lake. By October 9, two months after hostilities erupted, the war ended. In the end, fifteen hundred Dakota Sioux were taken prisoner, including many women and children. Over four hundred warriors were culled out of the group and tried before a military tribunal.

Military tribunals were something of a creature of the Civil War. Over 4,271 tribunals were held during the four years of the war in which just over 13,000 defendants were tried.[16] Military tribunals lacked statutory authority but flourished during the war. They existed outside of the legal system created by Congress. Their sole authority came from the president, who justified their legal jurisdiction under the "war powers" granted him under the Constitution.[17]

During wartime, belligerents abided by what were loosely called "the laws of war." These laws evolved over many years and determined what belligerents could and could not do while engaged in war. Individuals who violated these universally accepted laws were generally tried before military tribunals consisting of military officers who sat in judgment.[18]

The US government recognized the Dakota Sioux as a sovereign nation, which meant that the uprising by Dakota Sioux warriors was a legitimate war. Therefore, Dakota Sioux warriors who committed acts deemed in violation of the laws of war, such as killing noncombatant civilians, were lawfully triable by military tribunal. *General Orders, No. 100, Instructions for the Government of Armies of the United States in the Field,* states in paragraphs 22 and 23 that "the unarmed citizen is to be spared in person, property and honor as much as the exigencies of war will allow. . . . Private citizens are no longer murdered, enslaved or carried off."[19] While the Dakota warriors were probably unaware of General Orders 100, they were aware that women and children were noncombatants. It was the killing of women and children, as well as the documented atrocities, that became the basis for determining the death penalty following the military trials that soon took place. One such example comes from the testimony of trial witnesses against a Dakota Sioux named Cut-Nose. Cut-Nose "was found to have tomahawked to death 11 women and children as they huddled in wagons near the Beaver Creek settlement. Cut-Nose also, according to prosecution witnesses, snatched an infant from its mother's arms and riveted the small child to a fence, leaving it to die, writhing in agony."[20] Such accounts were not uncommon and only served to inflame passions throughout the trials and subsequent events.

Colonel Henry Sibley moved quickly and established a tribunal consisting of five military officers, all of whom had fought in the war. Four hundred Dakota men were designated by a three-member court of inquiry to stand trial for "murder, rape, and robbery." While the defendants, who had voluntarily turned themselves in, expressed concern over fair treatment, Sibley assured them the government only wanted to punish those individuals who committed crimes under the laws of war. Of course, none of those charged understood the laws of war, although they understood that women and children were noncombatants. Serving on the tribunal were Colonel William Crooks, Lieutenant Colonel William Marshall, Captain Hiram P. Grant, Captain Hiram S. Bailey, and Lieutenant Rollin C. Olin.[21]

The trials began on September 28 and lasted for several days. When it was over, 303 of the defendants were found guilty and sentenced to death by hanging. Just under one hundred were found not guilty. Although some of the defendants were clearly guilty of atrocities, the trial was a sham. The Indians were afforded no legal representation, and many were convicted on hearsay evidence or faulty eyewitness testimony. At least one defendant, Hdainyanka, maintained in a letter to his chief shortly before his execution that he had not "killed, wounded or injured a white man, or any white persons."[22] He professed complete innocence.

Once the trials ended, General Pope sent a telegram to President Lincoln informing him of the result, listing the names of the 303 Indians convicted, and their sentence of death by hanging. Without waiting for a response from Lincoln, both Pope and Sibley sent another telegram telling Lincoln that if he did not approve the sentencing there surely would be civil disorder and rioting followed by mob lynching of all 303 convicted men.[23] Lincoln responded immediately, much to the chagrin of Pope and Sibley, "Please forward, as soon as possible, the full and complete record of these convictions. And if the record does not fully indicate the more guilty and influential, of the culprits, please have a careful statement made on these points and forwarded to me. Send by mail. A. Lincoln."[24]

Lincoln's response created an uproar. Was he really going to review the trial transcript and alter the findings of the tribunal? Pope wrote to Lincoln a dire warning, "The people of this State, most of whom had relations or connections barbarously murdered and brutally outraged are exasperated to the last degree, and if the guilty are not all executed I think it nearly impossible to prevent the indiscriminant massacre of all Indians old men, women, and children."[25]

Episcopal Bishop Henry
Benjamin Whipple.
Wikimedia Commons.

Pope went on to point out that many of the soldiers had rela-
tives and friends who suffered, and military discipline was extremely fragile. If threats of mob violence and mass lynching were not
enough to persuade Lincoln to approve all 303 executions, Lincoln
was warned he would not receive a single vote in Minnesota in the
1864 presidential election.

Despite the continuing pleadings and threats coming from
Governor Ramsey, Colonel Sibley, and General Pope, Lincoln was determined to avert a bloodbath. Meeting with his judge advocate general, Joseph Holt, and supporting lawyers, Lincoln began going
through the trial records case by case. Lurking in the background
was the shadow of Bishop Benjamin Whipple. Whipple was a longtime friend and ally of the Dakota Sioux. He had written to Lincoln

over a year before the war broke out informing him of the poor treatment of the Indians and the corruption of the Indian Agency System. Whipple even traveled to Washington and met with Lincoln in the White House. He believed the entire Office of Indian Affairs was corrupt and brutalized the Indians it was meant to serve.

Whipple had come to the White House in September while the war still raged. One of his missions was to convince Lincoln that the whole corrupt system needed to be reformed. The war exacerbated the problem. Additionally, Whipple wanted Lincoln to know that many of the Dakota men actually helped save settlers by warning them of coming raids and helping to hide potential victims. Not all Dakota braves were on a killing rampage.

Whipple's entreaties to Lincoln likely had a deep effect. In his Annual Message to Congress on December 1, Lincoln reviewed the state of the nation. He spoke of the war, the blockade, the public lands, "the receipts into the treasury," and then he turned to the Indian problem in Minnesota:

> In the month of August last the Sioux Indians, in Minnesota, attacked the settlements in their vicinity with extreme ferocity, killing, indiscriminately, men, women, and children. This attack was wholly unexpected, and therefore, no means of defense had been provided. It is estimated that not less than eight hundred persons were killed by the Indians, and a large amount of property destroyed.[26]

And then Lincoln revealed the effect Bishop Whipple had on apprising him of the corrupt treatment of the Indians by adding, "I submit for your especial consideration whether our Indian system shall not be remodeled. Many wise and good men have impressed me with the belief that this can be profitably done."[27]

Five days later, on December 6, Lincoln released his decision on the tribunal's findings. Of the 303 cases reviewed, he found evidence in only thirty-nine that warranted the death penalty. He fo-

Artist rendition of the hanging of the thirty-eight Dakota Indians at Mankato, Minnesota, on December 26, 1862. Lithograph by John C. Wise, 1863.

cused only on those cases involving murder or rape of civilians. Along with his decision, Lincoln sent a list containing the names of the thirty-nine condemned, and asked that the executions be carried out on December 19. Sibley requested, and was granted, an extra week to prepare. In the interim, one of the accused was given a reprieve when it was determined, on further review, that he was innocent. This, in itself, suggests there was some attempt on the part of a few to be judicious in seeking justice.

On December 26 the executions were carried out. Hundreds of people showed up to witness the event. Several regiments of Minnesota troops surrounded the gallows to ensure no violence would mar the hanging. When it was over, Colonel Sibley sent a telegram to Lincoln: "I have the honor to inform you that 38 Indians and half-breeds ordered by you for execution were hung yesterday at Mankato, at 10 A.M. Everything went off quietly, and the other prisoners are well secured."[28]

In a letter to the US Senate, Lincoln informed the members of his actions:

> Anxious to not act with so much clemency as to encourage an-
> other outbreak on the one hand, nor with so much severity as to
> real cruelty on the other, I caused a careful examination of the
> records of the trials to be made, in view of first ordering the ex-
> ecution of such as had been proved guilty of violating females.
> Contrary to my expectations, only two of this class were found.
> I then directed a further examination, and a classification of all
> who were proven to have participated in *massacres*, as distin-
> guished from participation in *battles*. This class numbered for-
> ty, and included the two convicted of female violation. One of
> the number is strongly recommended by the Commission,
> which tried them, for commutation to ten years imprisonment
> [O-Ta-Kla, alias Godfrey]. I have ordered the other thirty-nine to
> be executed on Friday, the 19th instant.[29]

The Dakota trials and subsequent executions of the thirty-eight defendants[30] have given rise to modern-day condemnation. One of the
more egregious examples comes from an interview of Tiokasin
Ghosthorse on "First Voices Indigenous Radio" sponsored by the
Massachusetts School of Law. During his interview, Tiokasin
Ghosthorse described the hanging of thirty-eight Dakota men for
nothing more than shooting a settler's cow. Despite the fact that the
condemned claimed the cow lacked a brand or marking, Abraham
Lincoln still ordered their execution, he said. While this accusation
can be excused as a total ignorance of history, many examples cannot.

In his polemic on Abraham Lincoln (*Forced into Glory*), Lerone
Bennett leveled his attack on Lincoln as a racist by writing: "Although
Lincoln was famous for halting the execution of Union soldiers, he
approved one of the largest mass executions in military history [it
was, in fact, the largest mass execution in United States history]....
While the President expressed no attitude toward the Indian other

than to remember that one sneaked up behind his grandfather and killed him while he was working in a field, a double standard of race value might have had something to do with his treatment of the Sioux." This statement by Bennett is a complete misrepresentation of the known facts. No mention is made of Lincoln's examination of the trial records and his subsequent commuting the sentences of 265 condemned warriors. It suggests that Lincoln should have commuted all 303 defendants. To do otherwise reflects his racist attitude toward nonwhites, presumably influenced by the killing of his grandfather by an Indian.

Perhaps the most thorough account of the Dakota trials and executions comes from a university law professor. Carol Chomsky, a recognized scholar of legal history and a professor of law at the University of Minnesota Law School, wrote that the defendants "were convicted, not for the crime of murder, but for killings committed in warfare. The official review was conducted, not by an appellate court, but by the President of the United States."[31]

This, of course, is not what the defendants were convicted of—"killings committed in warfare." Lincoln, in fact, made sure that those among the accused who were warriors who only killed during battle were among the 265 men whose convictions he commuted.[32] The president sought to distinguish between "killing" and "massacres"—massacres being the killing of innocent women and children, noncombatants under any law of war.

In the section of her article describing the war, Professor Chomsky mentions the question of atrocities, dismissing them by writing, "In most cases, the Dakota killed the men and took the women and children prisoners. *Wild stories* [emphasis added] of mutilation by the Dakota in these encounters spread among the settlers, but historians have concluded that these reports were probably exaggerations of isolated instances of atrocities."[33] Chomsky's citation omits the names of any historians who claimed the reports were exaggerations. There are three books written on the uprising describing atrocities by Dakota warriors.[34]

Professor Chomsky dismisses the numerous personal accounts of atrocities and rape too lightly. The fact that she acknowledges "isolated instances of atrocities" can only mean that there were atrocities. The phrase "wild stories of mutilation" is hardly objective history. While there may well have been exaggerations of atrocities, and even some who lied in their descriptions, one cannot dismiss the eyewitness and personal accounts given, especially by women who saw their husbands and children murdered and were themselves raped. It simply challenges credulity to believe that a war that lasted over several weeks in which at least eight hundred white settlers were killed by roaming bands of hostile Dakota warriors did not involve the killing of women and children.

Chomsky writes: "Moreover, the Dakota, like other Indians, traditionally fought with methods substantially different from those of the American and Europeans. In particular, in intertribal Indian wars almost all members of the enemy nation—including women and children—were legitimate targets of attack, and captives were rarely taken. In arriving at its decisions, the Commission should have at least considered these differences in culture and military methods in any attempt to determine whether 'military necessity' permitted killing noncombatants in the war."[35] Chomsky seems to be saying that each side in the conflict may legally abide by its own rules of warfare, including the killing of women and children if it is part of their culture. The killing of both women and children during the uprising is well documented,[36] and by most nations' laws of war killing noncombatants such as women and children is forbidden. Such killing is a violation of the laws of war,[37] laws which the US military had enforced throughout the Civil War. It should be noted here that General Orders 100, a set of rules governing the conduct of the military, was not adopted until 1863, a year after the Minnesota uprising. However, the US military followed the traditional laws of war adopted from the British.

Professor Chomsky goes on to write, "The Dakota, therefore, should have been tried only on charges that they violated the customary rules of warfare, not for the civilian crimes of murder, rape, and robbery."[38] That is precisely what the defendants were charged with and convicted of, violating the laws of war by killing noncombatant women and children, leaving the atrocities aside.

The Dakota Sioux were recognized as a sovereign nation, and its soldiers were legitimate combatants of that nation. As such, their enemies quite legitimately expected them to abide by the laws of war. No Dakota soldier was convicted of killing a white combatant *during battle*. If any Dakota warriors were wrongly convicted, that is another matter. But to claim they were wrongly tried by military tribunal is simply incorrect. Had a Dakota Indian killed a white man tending his fields without provocation, that is murder, and triable in civilian court. Killing a noncombatant during wartime, such as a young child or infant, is murder, and triable by military tribunal.

Professor Chomsky writes, "The Dakota were a sovereign nation at war with the United States, and the men who fought the war were entitled to be treated as legitimate belligerents." She is correct in characterizing the Dakota men as "legitimate belligerents," which is why they were tried by military tribunal rather than civil court. If murder, rape, and robbery were committed, as most historians agree, how should the accused have been tried? Certainly not in civil court for crimes committed during war and in violation of the laws of war.

The trial may have been a sham. That defendants were not afforded counsel in every case, although counsel was provided in certain instances, was a violation of their rights. But while the trials may have been unfair, that does not negate the legal jurisdiction of a military tribunal. Nor does it mitigate the crimes for which the defendants were accused. The killing of unarmed civilians occurred, women as well as children. The rape of at least two women occurred. These constitute violations of the laws of war, and the civil code as well, and, importantly, violations of the standard code of human conduct adopted by most western nations in time of war.

Abraham Lincoln was deeply troubled by the Dakota War and the killings that occurred along the Minnesota frontier, on both sides. Deeply embroiled in a Civil War to preserve the Union, Lincoln devoted considerable time to reviewing each individual case of the condemned. He did this at the same time he received a series of angry protests threatening violence and mob lynching if he did not approve the execution of all 303 prisoners. It would have been easy for Lincoln to rubber-stamp the convictions and allow the hangings to go forward. After all, Indians did not have the right to vote. The only condemnation Lincoln would have received would be that of the clergy who attended the Indians during normal times.

Despite threats of violence and claims that he would lose his reelection bid in Minnesota in 1864, Lincoln followed his conscience and commuted the sentences of 265 of the condemned. He later wrote to Governor Ramsey, "I could not afford to hang men for votes."[39] In the end, the president granted reprieves to 265 condemned Dakota warriors while approving the sentences of thirty-eight. Lincoln's humanitarian act is ignored, condemning him instead for approving the execution of thirty-eight warriors.

The threatened loss of Minnesota's electoral votes in his bid for reelection in 1864 never materialized. Lincoln carried the state, winning the popular vote 25,060 to 17,375, a 7,685-vote plurality. While Minnesota's four electoral votes were a small part of Lincoln's 212 electoral vote victory, it must have proved especially gratifying to Lincoln that the people of Minnesota accepted compassionate justice over revenge.

In April 1863, four months after the executions, the Dakota Sioux were forcibly moved to the Dakota Territory, to what is now South Dakota. The prisoners Lincoln commuted were moved to Camp McClellan in Iowa. On March 22, 1866, President Andrew Johnson ordered their release. They were then moved to the Santee Reservation in Nebraska. Little Crow, the leader of the Dakota Sioux, along with more than 150 followers, fled to Canada only to eventually return to Minnesota, where Little Crow was shot and killed by a local farmer on July 3, 1863, while picking berries with his son.[40] To many Minnesotans, final justice had been served.

The city of Mankato has established a memorial, Reconciliation Park, calling for healing and forgiveness. Every year Dakota Sioux Native Americans hold a memorial ride honoring the memory of the thirty-eight Dakota men executed.

Freedom to the Slaves by Currier and Ives, 1862. Edward Steers Jr. collection.

6   The Reluctant Emancipator

If Lincoln had had his way, there would be no blacks in America. None.

Lerone Bennett, Forced into Glory

In an article appearing in the *Papers of the Abraham Lincoln Association*, Kent State University professor John T. Hubbell described the unending debate surrounding Abraham Lincoln and emancipation. Hubbell wrote that what might be described as the "civil rights period" beginning in the 1960s has led "to a reevaluation of Lincoln—from the great emancipator to the reluctant emancipator to the white supremacist, or in more vulgar terms, Lincoln was just another honkie."[1]

While Hubbell's article appeared in 1980, the mischaracterization of Lincoln, in certain quarters, continues to this day. In an op-ed piece in the November 21, 2018, *Washington Post* on the controversy surrounding Robert E. Lee, titled "Good Riddance," US Army general Stanley McChrystal wrote, "It takes nothing away from Abraham Lincoln's heroic stewardship of our nation through the Civil War, for instance, to admit that he was still a creature of his era. For most of his career, he saw slaves as rival laborers for white wage-workers and thought they should go back to Africa."[2]

Wow! Where did General McChrystal learn that piece of non-history? Hopefully not at West Point. By the time Lincoln became president there were 4.4 million African Americans in the United

States, of whom 3.9 million were slaves. The importation of slaves had ended in 1808, which means nearly all of the 3.9 million slaves had been born in the United States, not Africa. Sending them "back to Africa" shows a clear lack of knowledge of history, as well as logistics.

While the *Dred Scott* decision by the US Supreme Court in 1857 ruled that blacks were not US citizens, subsequent rulings reversed that decision and gave blacks born in the United States full citizenship.[3] Does anyone think that a person with Lincoln's intellect, and political savvy, believed he could deport 4.4 million African Americans to Africa? It is nonsensical. We can forgive General McChrystal since he is not a Lincoln scholar, but he might have checked with a scholar before writing such misinformation in his article.

To be fair to the general, Lincoln did support limited colonization during the early years of his presidency. But, it is essential that we examine Lincoln's colonization views critically in their entirety before we claim he wanted to send all blacks "back to Africa."

Somewhat in tune with McChrystal's "back to Africa" statement, Lerone Bennett, in his book *Forced into Glory*, wrote, "If Lincoln had had his way, there would be no Blacks in America. None!" Lincoln's real purpose as president was not to free the slaves, Bennett claimed, but to prolong slavery until he could put a plan in place to deport all blacks to a foreign shore. Bennett writes: "[Lincoln] did everything he could to deport Blacks and to make America a Great White Place."[4]

By selecting Lincoln's words carefully and placing his own interpretation on their meaning, Mr. Bennett is able to weave an ugly view of Abraham Lincoln that turns history on its ear and furthers the latest revisionist theory that Lincoln was a white supremacist. The colonization theme is another myth along with those claiming that Booth escaped and Edwin Stanton was behind Lincoln's murder.

Lincoln faced multiple problems, all traceable to the institution of slavery. In 1860, of the 2 billion acres that comprised the United States, 900 million, or just under half, consisted of the territories. Allowing slavery in this new region would nearly double the land available for slavery, thereby dramatically increasing the need for new slaves. Lincoln recognized the problems this could cause and stood firm against the expansion of slavery into the territories, as did the newly formed Republican Party. While states controlled the laws within their own borders, deciding whether they would be slave or free, Congress controlled the territories, and here was the battle-ground. Lincoln believed that to ban slavery in the territories was to put it on the road to ultimate extinction.

Lincoln also believed that to abolish slavery where it already existed without some form of compensation would seriously disrupt the South's economy. Lincoln was keenly aware of this. Cotton was king, and 70 percent of the South's economy came from the export of cotton to Europe. Prior to the war, Southern cotton accounted for 78 percent of the cotton used by British mills, and 90 percent of the cotton consumed by French mills. By 1860, cotton sales brought over $100 million in sales to the South (equal to $2.3 billion today).[5]

Shortly before the war began, James Hammond of South Carolina proclaimed, "Old England would topple headlong and carry the whole civilized world with her. No, you dare not make war on cotton. Cotton is king."[6] If cotton was king, then slavery was queen. The South's cotton fields were tilled, planted, and harvested by slaves. To Southerners, Lincoln would not only destroy the South's economy, he would unleash 250 years of black revenge on Southern masters.

On Christmas Eve 1860, Alabama's secession commissioner, Stephen Fowler Hale, addressed the legislature of Kentucky on secession. Hale stated that the election of Abraham Lincoln was "a culmination of aggravated outrage, which no Southern patriot could mistake or fail to understand . . . the extinction of slavery." Hale pointed out that it was a question of safety. "Yankee fanaticism" had become "an unchained demon."[7] Hale got it right. The election of

James Henry Hammond.
Wikimedia Commons.

Stephen F. Hale. Alabama
Department of Archives and
History.

Abraham Lincoln would lead to the extinction of slavery, and Southern slave owners knew it.

Slaves have a direct relationship with the land. As the slave population increases, so must the land if both are to keep their value. The slave population was increasing at a rate of 50,000 to 60,000 births per year during the 1850s, an increase of over 600,000 for the decade. Most slave owners had the necessary slaves to work their plantations. This increasing number of slaves created a financial burden on slave owners. New slaves required food, lodging, clothing, and a certain amount of care. The solution was to sell off your excess slaves, but if the market saw an increase in available slaves it would see a decrease in their value. Market conditions controlled the value of slaves as property. The more slaves, the less their value.

The solution to this growing problem was expansion—new land, new plantations. Increase the number of acres of land available for farming, and the demand for slaves will go up, thereby relieving the financial burden of existing slave owners and maintaining the value of their own slaves and land. This is the precise cause of the problem, and it was growing every year. Thus the demands to allow slavery into the territories were growing by the year. There were related calls for a "filibuster" to seize Mexican lands. George Washington Lafayette Bickley formed the Knights of the Golden Circle in the mid-1850s with the goal of colonizing the northern part of Mexico, thereby annexing the land and expanding slave territory. By Lincoln's election Bickley's plan shifted to secession and supporting the new Confederate states.

Lincoln not only faces revisionist characterizations of the likes of Stephen Hale and Lerone Bennett, but a group of modern-day historians who are critical of Lincoln's policies and alleged beliefs on race. His actions belied his words. He acted too slowly on emancipation, and did not believe in racial equality, they say. He favored colonization, and to believe Lerone Bennett, he wanted to deport, forci-

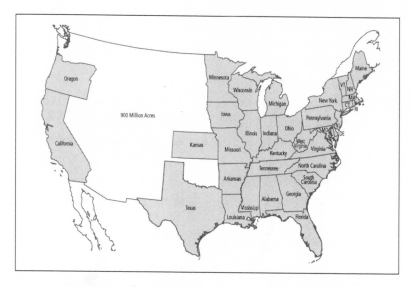

During the Civil War, the United States consisted of 2 billion acres of land, of which 900 million acres were in the territories. It was in the territories where Southern slave interests desperately wanted to expand slavery. Map courtesy of Kieran McAuliffe.

bly if necessary, all of the blacks in America. All are mischaracterizations of Lincoln's position. The problem, as Richard Striner has pointed out in his book *Lincoln and Race,* is that "Lincoln's documented words on the matter of race can be read in opposite ways."[8]

Bennett, and like-minded people, wrote as if Abraham Lincoln held the power to abolish slavery at any time he chose. Bennett is wrong. Neither the president nor the Congress of the United States had the power to abolish slavery by executive order or by legislation. Slavery was protected by the Constitution, and the only way to abolish the peculiar institution legally was by amending the Constitution. That, of course, happened in December 1865, and it happened because of Lincoln's political will, not reluctantly, and not by pressure from slaves or abolitionists.

Seemingly supportive of Lincoln's detractors are his own

words from the debates with Stephen Douglas during the 1858 senatorial campaign in Illinois. In their first meeting in Ottawa, LaSalle
County, Illinois, on August 21, 1858, Lincoln said:

> I will say here, while upon this subject, that I have no purpose
> directly or indirectly to interfere with the institution of slav-
> ery in the States where it exists. I believe I have no lawful
> right to do so, and I have no inclination to do so. I have no pur-
> pose to introduce political and social equality between the
> white and the black races. There is a physical difference be-
> tween the two, which in my judgment will probably forever
> forbid their living together upon the footing of perfect equali-
> ty, and inasmuch as it becomes a necessity that there must be
> a difference, I, as well as Judge Douglas, am in favor of the race
> to which I belong, having the superior position. But, I hold not
> withstanding all this, there is no reason in the world why the
> negro is not entitled to all the natural rights enumerated in
> the Declaration of Independence, the right to life, liberty, and
> the pursuit of happiness.[9]

These words are often turned against Lincoln to support the view
that he was a white supremacist. Lincoln's policy, however, was
against the extension of slavery. He took the least racist position that
would not lose him the support of his racist neighbors. The eminent
Lincoln historian Don E. Fehrenbacher wrote that "if Lincoln had responded differently [to Douglas's question on black equality] during
the debates, the Lincoln of history simply would not exist."[10] Lincoln
took the middle road between Douglas and the abolitionists. He did
so in an effort to win election to the U.S. Senate, where he hoped he
might make a difference.

   As a prelude to amending the Constitution to abolish slavery,
which would not come for another three years, Lincoln decided to
issue a proclamation declaring slaves held within those areas in rebellion "thenceforward and forever free." How could he do this if the
Constitution protected slavery? He did it by turning to the war pow-

Engraving by Alexander H. Ritchie (1864) of Francis Bicknell Carpenter's painting of the first reading of the Emancipation Proclamation by Lincoln to his cabinet. Library of Congress.

ers granted the president under the Constitution. These powers allow the commander in chief to take certain steps to injure the enemy, and lessen his ability to wage war.[11] While slaves did not serve in the Confederate army, they supported its efforts in numerous ways. If slaves were property, as Southern politicians claimed, then confiscating them (by setting them free) was legal under the war powers of the president.

Lincoln's proclamation did not free slaves in those areas under Union control because Lincoln had no Constitutional authority, or war powers authority, to free them in loyal territory. The Emancipation Proclamation's justification was as a military order designed to hurt the enemy, plain and simple. A careful reading of the Constitution as well as Lincoln's lengthy explanation of his action would have helped Bennett to understand this important point.

Bennett goes to great length to show that the proclamation did not free a single slave, writing, "Lincoln deliberately drafted the document so it wouldn't free a single Negro immediately. What Lincoln did—and it was so clever that we ought to stop calling him honest Abe—was to 'free' slaves in Confederate-held territory where he couldn't free them and to leave them in slavery in Union-held territory where he could have freed them."[12]

This comment shows a complete lack of understanding of the Constitution and presidential powers at the time. Bennett is correct in concluding that the Emancipation Proclamation freed few if any slaves under Confederate control, freeing only those slaves in Southern states under Union control. It did encourage slaves to run away and seek refuge within Union army lines. The Confiscation Act of 1862, often cited by people like Bennett as the "real emancipation act," didn't free many slaves either, and it wasn't likely to free them.[13] This act declared that the slaves of any citizen who actively supported the rebellion could be confiscated and set free. The catch, however, required such "liberation" to be adjudicated in the federal courts, case by case. Because private property is protected under the Constitution, "confiscating" slaves had to be sanctioned by a court after a full hearing. There were over 380,000 slave owners in the South, and if each had his or her day in court, we would still be trying cases today while all other court business stood still. The courts would be clogged into the twenty-first century.

Slavery would end only through force: political and physical force, and Lincoln commanded both. When the US House of Representatives failed to pass the Thirteenth Amendment in the summer of 1864, Lincoln rolled up his sleeves and began twisting a few arms. He instructed the chairman of the Republican Party to make sure the amendment was part of the party platform. The pro-slavery Democratic platform was silent on the issue.

The fall elections would produce a new House that would guarantee passage in the next Congress. Lincoln didn't wait. He used his persuasive powers to convince thirteen Democrats who had voted against the amendment to change their votes. They did, and the amendment passed in the lame duck House, gaining the necessary two-thirds majority. This was not the action of a reluctant president who sought to delay emancipation until he could develop a plan to deport all blacks.

On the question of colonization, Bennett correctly points out that Lincoln was a supporter of colonization, but of limited colonization, and only voluntary. Bennett characterizes Lincoln's view as "forced deportation," writing, "He [Lincoln] did everything he could to deport Blacks and to make America a Great White Place."[14]

In one instance Lincoln had approved a contract with an unscrupulous businessman to set up a colony on Île-à-Vache, an island off the coast of Haiti.[15] When Lincoln learned that several hundred blacks had been abandoned without proper support, he ordered the US Navy to bring them back to the United States. If Lincoln's plan were to rid the country of blacks by deportation, he showed poor judgment in returning those blacks who had already been "deported." Here was his opportunity to make America a little whiter. It was Lincoln's last effort in colonizing blacks.

Supporting colonization is not the same as preferring it. Lincoln believed it was one small answer to the larger problem confronting blacks in a racist society. In a speech in Peoria, Illinois, in 1854, Lincoln stated the following regarding colonization:

> If all earthly power were given to me, I should not know what to do, as to the existing institution [slavery]. My first impulse would be to free all the slaves and send them to Liberia[16]—to their own native land. But a moment's reflection would convince me that, whatever of high hope (as I think there is) there may be in this in the long run, its sudden execution is impossible. If they were all landed there in a day, they would all perish in the next ten days; and there are not surplus shipping and

surplus money enough in the world to carry them there in many times ten days.[17]

What readers of *Forced into Glory* should know is that Lincoln advocated *voluntary* colonization, not *forced*. No black was forced to leave the country against his or her free will. Only those who wanted to leave were offered the opportunity. The great majority declined; only a few did not.

Lincoln's so-called colonization policy was a ploy more than a policy. He attempted to address the slavery problem by offering compensated emancipation, and was roundly rebuffed. At the very moment he was preparing to release his Emancipation Proclamation he signed a contract for colonizing five hundred blacks. It too failed. Lincoln then pulled the trigger and issued his Preliminary Proclamation, as if to say, "I tried other measures and they failed. The Emancipation Proclamation will not fail."

Whatever Lincoln believed in his heart regarding social equality, he believed slavery was morally wrong, and he said so on numerous occasions: "If slavery is not wrong, nothing is wrong."[18] As early as 1837, while an Illinois state legislator, Lincoln was one of only six legislators to vote against proslavery resolutions; seventy-seven voted in favor of the legislation. One of the more oft-quoted statements of Lincoln concerning slavery comes from a letter he wrote on August 22, 1862, to Horace Greeley, the publisher and editor of the *New York Tribune*. The *Tribune*, which published Greeley's editorials, was among the most widely read newspapers in the country. Greeley, a Republican and early supporter of Lincoln, became critical of Lincoln's efforts to curry the favor of the border state politicians for fear of losing these critical states to the Confederacy.

Lincoln considered the border states of Kentucky, Missouri, Maryland, and Delaware critical to winning the war. In a letter to his Illinois friend, Orville Browning, Lincoln wrote, "I think to lose Kentucky is nearly the same as to lose the whole game. Kentucky gone, we cannot hold Missouri, nor, as I think, Maryland. These all against us, and the job on our hands is too large for us. We would as well consent to separation at once, including the surrender of this capitol."[19] These four slave states remained loyal to the Union although closely tied to the Confederacy in many ways. Greeley wrongly felt that Lincoln pandered to the border state politicians, and their strong support of slavery.

In an editorial published in the *Tribune* on August 19, 1862, titled "The Prayer of Twenty Millions," Greeley took Lincoln to task for not emancipating the slaves, knowing full well he lacked such power constitutionally. Greeley wrote, "Had you, Sir, in your Inaugural Address, unmistakably given notice that, in case the Rebellion already commenced were persisted in, and your efforts to preserve the Union and enforce the laws should be resisted by armed force, you would recognize no loyal person as rightfully held in slavery by a traitor, we believe the Rebellion would therein have received a staggering if not fatal blow." Greeley went on to write, "What an immense majority of the Loyal Millions of your countrymen require of you is a frank, declared, unqualified, ungrudging execution of the laws of the land more especially of the Confiscation Act."[20]

Lincoln responded to Greeley's editorial with a letter dated August 22, 1862. Rather than attack or alienate his critic, Lincoln responds as if to a friend. Lincoln leaves no doubt as to his policy:

> I would save the Union. I would save it the shortest way under the Constitution. The sooner the national authority can be restored, the nearer the Union will be "the Union as it was." If there be those that would not save the Union, unless they could not at the same time save slavery, I do not agree with them. If there be those that would not save the Union unless they could at the same time destroy slavery, I do not agree with them. My paramount object in this struggle is to save the Union, and is not either to save or destroy slavery. If I could save the Union without freeing any slave I would do it, and if I could save it by

Horace Greeley. Photograph by
Mathew B. Brady, 1864. Edward
Steers Jr. collection.

freeing all the slaves I would do it; and if I could save it by freeing some and leaving others alone I would also do that. What I
do about slavery, and the colored race, I do because I believe it
helps to save the Union; and what I forbear, I forbear because I
do not believe it should help to save the Union. I shall do less
whenever I shall believe what I am doing hurts the cause, and I
shall do more whenever I believe doing more will help the
cause. I shall try to correct errors when shown to be errors; and
I shall adopt new views so fast as they shall appear to be true
views. I have here stated my purpose according to my view of
official duty, and I intend no modification of my oft-expressed
personal wish that all men everywhere could be free.

Yours, A. Lincoln

It is in these words, written by Lincoln, that some historians view him
as the "reluctant Emancipator." But, as Phillip Shaw Paludan has
pointed out, Lincoln was not a "reluctant" but a "cautious" emancipa-

tor. On July 22, 1862, a full month earlier than his letter to Greeley, Lincoln informed his cabinet of his decision to issue his Emancipation Proclamation. In that seminal moment, Lincoln linked saving the Union with emancipation. Rather than choosing between union or emancipation, he chose both.

Although Lincoln's proclamation freed few slaves in areas under Confederate control, it established a reason for fighting the war. The Declaration of Independence didn't free a single American when it was released on July 4, 1776. It took a war to do that. But the Declaration of Independence established the principles under which that war would be fought, and freedom would be won. In a similar vein, the Emancipation Proclamation did not free many slaves, but it did establish the principles under which the Civil War would be fought and freedom would be won. This is an important point to understand that seems lost on Lincoln's critics.

Lincoln's views were well known to Southern leaders, which is why they rejected his presidency. When Confederate peace commissioners met at Hampton Roads in 1865, Lincoln was willing to entertain terms of peace and reunion, but only on the condition that abolishing slavery was not a negotiating point. Lincoln insisted that any peace proposal include ratification of the Thirteenth Amendment banning slavery. Three days before his death, he proposed suffrage for certain blacks. From the earliest moment in 1837 until his death in 1865, Lincoln stood resolutely against slavery, and for equal rights for blacks. At each step along the tortuous path leading to freedom and full citizenship, Lincoln was ahead of the nation, pulling it along the path to freedom. He was anything but a "reluctant emancipator."

Abraham Lincoln has become a universal symbol of human ideals. Toppling such an icon is not an easy task. Anyone who seeks to bring down Lincoln will have to do more than cry fraud. Putting dreams in Lincoln's head (Lincoln dreamed of making "America a Great White Place")[21] or putting someone else's words in his mouth[22] will not do the job. While it may titillate the few, it will not convince the many.

In his speech from the White House balcony on April 11, 1865, Lincoln began moving the country forward in the only way that would ensure success—he advocated black suffrage in small, sure steps. Lincoln said, "It is also unsatisfactory to some that the elective franchise is not given to the colored man. I would myself prefer that it were now conferred on the very intelligent, and on those who serve our cause as soldiers."[23] No amount of drum beating by Bennett can diminish the revolutionary significance of this statement.

While it is important to focus on what Abraham Lincoln did as opposed to what he said, it would do those who feel Lincoln did not do enough fast enough to heed Lincoln's words to his young law partner, Billy Herndon: "History is not history unless it is the truth."[24]

This haunting photograph of Abraham Lincoln taken by Alexander Gardner on February 5, 1865, shows the terrible toll the war took on Lincoln and his health. Library of Congress.

7 | The Ailing Lincoln

> If any personal description of me is thought desirable, it
> may be said, I am, in height, six feet, four inches, nearly;
> lean in flesh, weighing, on average one hundred and eighty
> pounds; dark complexion, with coarse black hair, and grey
> eyes—no other marks or brands recollected.
>
> Yours very truly, A. Lincoln
—Letter to Jesse Fell, December 20, 1859

Thus, Abraham Lincoln left us with a terse description of himself, devoid of any comment as to his health or well-being. His anatomy was unusual and caused people to comment, often unflatteringly. His best friend in his early adulthood, Joshua Speed, described him in a letter to William Herndon following Lincoln's death: "He was a long, gawky, ugly, shapeless, man."[1] Herndon, his close friend and law partner of twenty-one years, gave a detailed description of Lincoln in his biographical study that is worth repeating here:

> He was thin, wiry, sinewy, raw-boned; thin through the breast
> to the back, and narrow across the shoulders; standing he
> leaned forward—was what may be called stoop-shouldered, in-
> clining to the consumptive by build. His usual weight was one
> hundred and eighty pounds. . . . When he walked he moved cau-
> tiously but firmly; his long arms and giant hands swung down
> by his side. He walked with an even tread, the inner sides of his
> feet being parallel. He put the whole foot flat down on the
> ground at once, not landing on the heel; he likewise lifted his

foot all at once, not rising from the toe, and hence he had no spring to his walk.[2]

Robert Wilson, who in 1836 was elected to the Illinois House of Representatives along with Lincoln and became one of the famous "Long Nine" legislators, wrote, "His legs were long, feet large; arms long, longer than any man I ever knew, when standing straiht [sic], and letting his arms fall down his sides, the points of his fingers would touch a point lower on his legs by nearly three inches than was usual with other persons . . . his hands were large and bony."[3]

It was these unusual traits that attracted the attention of several modern-day clinicians. Early in the 1960s, two physicians, independently, started a medical snowball that rolled down Lincoln's hill and continues to this day. Both men claimed Lincoln suffered from a rare disease known as Marfan syndrome. Their diagnosis was eventually followed by others claiming Lincoln suffered from constipation, multiple endocrine neoplasia 2b (a rare form of cancer), and mercury poisoning. Had Lincoln not been assassinated by John Wilkes Booth in April 1865, these diagnosticians claim, he would not have survived his second term as president. The claim lacks factual evidence and is based on dubious suppositions. It is part of the revisionist lure so attractive to those who choose to rewrite Lincoln's history.

Marfan syndrome is a disorder of the body's connective tissue. It causes skeletal, ocular, and cardiovascular problems. Connective tissue is tissue that connects, supports, or binds other tissues in the body and the body's organs. A person's lenses (eyes) may become detached, their major artery, the aorta, may become weak and eventually rupture, and they may also experience a form of emphysema due to damage to their lungs. The disease can be terribly debilitating. It is a genetic disease carried on one of the autosomal chromosomes (not the sex-determining X and Y chromosomes), and while the syndrome is inherited from one or both parents, approximately 15 percent of Marfan cases are due to spontaneously arising mutations that were not transmitted by either parent.

In 1964, Harold Schwartz, an instructor in medicine at the University of Southern California School of Medicine in Los Angeles, published an article in the *Journal of the American Medical Association (JAMA)* titled "Abraham Lincoln and the Marfan Syndrome." In his summation Schwartz wrote: "The Marfan syndrome was found in a male descendant of Mordecai Lincoln II, great-great-grandfather of Abraham Lincoln. The common ancestry of the patient and the 16th president appears to establish genealogically that Lincoln's unusual morphological characteristics were manifestations of the genetically determined arrangement of connective tissue described by Marfan in 1896."[4]

Dr. Schwartz was drawn to Abraham Lincoln as a possible candidate for Marfan disease when he treated a Marfan patient who he later determined was of the Lincoln lineage. The patient was descended from Mordecai Lincoln II. Dr. Schwartz was struck by the physical description of Lincoln given by many of those who knew him best. The physical description given at the beginning of this chapter can be considered to be accurate and, therefore, the legitimate subject of medical analysis.

Dr. Schwartz presents a partial genealogical tree for eleven generations of the Lincoln family descended from Samuel Lincoln (1619–1690), the American progenitor who immigrated to North America in 1637 from Hingham, England. In his genealogical tree, Dr. Schwartz lists thirty-five individuals (twenty-nine males and six females), of whom two are suspected to have Marfan syndrome, Abraham Lincoln and "Case 1," Dr. Schwartz's patient who was diagnosed as having Marfan syndrome in 1959. Eliminating Lincoln leaves only Case 1.

Of the twenty-nine male descendants of Samuel Lincoln, twelve are listed as bearing a "morphological resemblance" to President

Lincoln, and three with *forme fruste*. *Forme fruste* is a medical term derived from Latin meaning "to be mistaken" or "to be confused." In modern medicine, *forme fruste* is an atypical or attenuated expression of a disease, with the implications of incompleteness, partial presence. In other words, "maybe."[5] Two individuals are listed as "suspect *forme fruste*," Thomas Lincoln, the president's father, and Robert Lincoln, the president's son. Both of these men show no similarity to Abraham Lincoln in their physical anatomy, leaving one to wonder just what was the basis for diagnosing them as *forme fruste*.

Dr. Schwartz's elaborate genealogical tree lists "scattered kin of Lincoln with characteristics similar to the greatest of their line as would be expected in a genetic entity known to be of an irregularly dominant type of inheritance."[6] Schwartz's statement that "scattered kin of Lincoln with characteristics similar to the greatest of their line" is curious. Schwartz lists four citations that relate to Lincoln's ancestors, none of which give any physical description of any kin prior to Thomas Lincoln, the president's father. A single photograph of Thomas Lincoln exists, and its provenance is suspect. Today, most historians simply refer to the photograph as "traditional."

Even so, Thomas Lincoln bore no resemblance to his son physically. Dennis Hanks, Lincoln's second cousin, who lived for four years in Thomas Lincoln's cabin, described Thomas in a letter to William Herndon: "He was a large man of great muscular power his usual weight 196 pounds I have weighed him many a time. He was 5 feet 10 inches high and *well proportioned* [emphasis added] . . . though not a fleshy man he was built so compact that it was difficult to find or feel a rib in his body—a muscular man his equal I never saw."[7] This description bears little similarity to that of Abraham Lincoln save for the term "muscular." More importantly, it bears no similarity to a *forme fruste* individual.

Of the twenty-five male members of the Lincoln lineage, Schwartz describes twelve of them as having a "morphological resemblance" to the president, including his four sons. How is this possible when little or no information exists on their health or their anatomy beyond birth and death dates? Eddy Lincoln died just short of his fourth birthday. Willie Lincoln died at the age of eleven from typhoid fever. None of the four sons bore any of the unusual physical characteristics that Schwartz ascribes to Lincoln: "extremities were disproportionately long, fingers were elongated and bony, unusually large feet, skin was leathery and sallow, the eyelids were heavy with a tendency to droop, a chest so thin as to have been described by Herndon as a 'sunken breast.'"[8] It is true that Robert Lincoln suffered from vision problems, as did Thomas Lincoln late in life, but there is no evidence it was caused by detached retinas, which are typical of Marfan syndrome.

Schwartz builds his case on his patient, "Case 1," eight generations removed from Mordecai II, Abraham Lincoln's great-great-grandfather. Schwartz supports his claim that Lincoln suffered from Marfan syndrome by comparing Lincoln's unusual anatomy to that of his patient, Case 1, a young boy diagnosed with Marfan syndrome, ergo, Lincoln had Marfan. Schwartz finishes off his analysis by discussing personality traits. Quoting Carl Sandburg, Schwartz points out that people often described Lincoln by referring to "his unusual appearance, his sense of humor and kindliness, his sadness, his readiness to learn, and his willingness to be of help."[9] Schwartz then cites two British clinicians who describe their own Marfan patient in a 1918 British journal: "He was always undernourished but was sensitive and mentally advanced for his age, with a quaint way of expressing himself and a sense of humor of his own."[10] Schwartz concludes, "A more succinct and specific characterization of the known Lincoln personality and uniqueness of expression would be difficult to formulate."[11] It would also apply to millions of persons throughout the world.

Schwartz's entire case centers on two points: Lincoln's unusual anatomy, which bears similarity to that of many Marfan patients, and a young boy diagnosed with Marfan syndrome who shares a common ancestor with Lincoln over eight generations. To invoke twelve members of the Lincoln extended lineage with a "morphological resemblance" to Lincoln is baffling. In over forty years of studying the ancestral family of Abraham Lincoln, I have yet to find any physical description of any member of Lincoln's family prior to his father, Thomas. The references cited by Schwartz in support of his genealogical tree simply do not contain any physical descriptions of any members of the Lincoln family tree that would allow an "Inferential Lincoln-Marfan Pedigree."

The only evidence we have are the numerous descriptions of Lincoln by those who knew him, the over 120 photographs that show us what he looked like, two life masks and casts of his hands, and the autopsy report following his assassination. In addition, we have two pairs of Lincoln's eyeglasses from when he was president, which are ordinary reading glasses. The diopter measurement was determined as +1.62 for each eye for one pair of glasses, and +2.00 for each eye for a second pair. Both pairs of glasses were in Lincoln's coat pocket at the time of his assassination.[12] These glasses suggest Lincoln's only visual problem was presbyopia. Presbyopia is the gradual loss of your eyes' ability to focus on nearby objects. It is a common occurrence with aging.

While Dr. Schwartz discusses those aspects of Lincoln's anatomy that support his claim that Lincoln suffered from Marfan disease, he fails to discuss those traits displayed by Lincoln that refute his claim. Marfan syndrome is often characterized by an individual's appearing tall and slender with disproportionally long arms, legs, and fingers, extreme nearsightedness, and flat feet. All of these conditions do pertain to Lincoln to some degree, and have been used by the proponents of Lincoln to support their claim that he had Marfan. But these same proponents, including Dr. Schwartz, overlook or ignore the other side of that coin—in particular, Lincoln's legendary strength. William Herndon, his law partner and friend, described an unusually strong Lincoln: "Mr. Lincoln's remarkable strength resulted not so much from muscular power as from the toughness of his sinews. He could not only lift from the ground enormous weight, but could throw a cannon-ball or a maul farther than anyone else in New Salem."[13]

Herndon continued his description of Lincoln's amazing strength: "By an arrangement of ropes and straps, harnessed about his hips, he was enabled one day at the mill [New Salem's grist and sawmill] to astonish a crowd of village celebrities by lifting a box of stones weighing near a thousand pounds. There is no fiction either in the story that he lifted a barrel of whiskey from the ground and drank from the bung."[14]

Lincoln's abilities as an athlete cannot be overlooked. His fame as a wrestler is legion. His famous match with Jack Armstrong in New Salem is well documented, but Lincoln was also challenged during the Black Hawk War and proved his athletic ability by consistently beating his challengers. In addition to accounts of Lincoln's exceptional strength is his age. Two studies carried out in the 1970s reported that the mean age at death of 417 Marfan patients was forty-one years and thirty-two years, respectively.[15] Lincoln died at age fifty-six, well past the average age of death in these two studies, and he died from a gunshot wound.

In Lincoln's day the disease was unknown (went undiagnosed) and lacked any treatment. Depending on the severity of the disease, it is doubtful Lincoln would have lived much past forty. Nathaniel Grigsby, a neighbor when Lincoln lived in Indiana, wrote to William Herndon in response to Herndon's inquiry, "He was always in good health—never sick—had an Excellent Constitution—& took Care of it."[16]

By Dr. Schwartz's own reckoning, of the thirty-five individuals listed in his "Lincoln-Marfan Pedigree," only two are shown as having the disease, Abraham Lincoln and Case 1. Dismissing Lincoln from this pedigree, only one has actually been diagnosed with Marfan. Lincoln's physical condition, legendary strength, and age all dispute Dr. Schwartz's conclusion. Whatever Lincoln's medical problems were, Marfan's syndrome was not among them.

MEN 2b: Multiple Endocrine Neoplasia

In 2008, Dr. John G. Sotos, a Johns Hopkins–trained physician and the CEO of Apneos Corporation, entered the Lincoln medical merry-go-round by claiming Abraham Lincoln suffered from a rare form of cancer known by clinicians as MEN 2b (multiple endocrine neoplasia). He put his diagnosis forward in a book titled *The Physical Lincoln*.[17]

The National Cancer Institute, one of several institutes in the National Institutes of Health, describes multiple endocrine neoplasia 2B (MEN 2b) as: "A rare, genetic disorder that affects the endocrine glands and causes a type of thyroid cancer called medullary thyroid cancer, pheochromocytoma, and parathyroid gland cancer. It may also cause benign (noncancerous) tumors in the adrenal glands and growths around the nerves in the lips, tongue, lining of the mouth, and eyelids. Gastrointestinal symptoms and trouble with the spine or bones in the feet and thighs may also occur. MEN2B syndrome is caused by a mutation in a gene called RET."[18] Dr. Sotos was struck by what he, and Drs. Gorden and Schwartz, saw as Lincoln's "Marfanoid" appearance. In examining photographs of Lincoln's face, he claims to have seen four "masses" or lumps "on or near Lincoln's lips." Sotos goes on to explain that these lumps, or "balls," accumulate to such a degree in patients with MEN 2b that they enlarge the lips. This feature is a characteristic of the disease, and when linked to Lincoln's Marfan-like anatomy, bushy eyebrows, and slumped nature when seated, it led Dr. Sotos to conclude that Lincoln "unmistakably shows, however, that MEN 2B has the potential

The Two Lincolns. The photograph on the left was taken by Alexander Hesler four months prior to Lincoln's election as president. The photograph on the right was taken in 1865 by Alexander Gardner four and a half years later. The change in Lincoln's appearance is dramatic. Library of Congress.

to unify an astonishing number of Lincoln's features under one root cause."[19] That one root cause, according to Dr. Sotos, is multiple endocrine neoplasia 2b.

This disease is a systemic disease affecting many parts of the body, including several organs. It is the result of a dominant autosomal gene, meaning that if Lincoln carried the gene the likelihood of two of his sons manifesting the disease is high. The disease is extremely rare. It is estimated that only 1 out of 600,000 people have the disease. In 2001, 150 cases were reported in the medical literature.[20] Age is another problem in Dr. Sotos's diagnosis. Without any treatment, such as thyroidectomy, the average life expectancy is twenty-one years.[21]

As Dr. Sotos points out, diagnosis today is not a problem since DNA testing for the causative gene is available. No such test existed in Lincoln's day. Since Lincoln himself is not available, diagnosis must be based on descriptions of Lincoln in the literature, and photographic images.[22] Since MEN 2b is characterized by medullary thyroid carcinoma (cancer of the thyroid gland), removal of the thyroid gland is among the modern treatments to prolong the life of the patient. Since MEN 2b was not discovered as a disease until the 1960s, thyroidectomy was not an option in Lincoln's day.

Recently, Dr. Sotos has undertaken an attempt to acquire and analyze Lincoln's DNA in a search for the MEN 2b gene. While putting a great deal of effort into his research, Dr. Sotos has come up dry. Of the several samples tested, none have a proven provenance, and those that gave sequence results did not contain the peculiar segment of DNA associated with the MEN 2b gene. Dr. Sotos's effort, however, is the right one, because both Marfan syndrome and MEN 2b are genetic diseases caused by single genes. The sequencing of Lincoln's DNA, if it ever occurs, would provide unquestioned proof of whether Lincoln suffered from one or both of these diseases.

Physician diagnoses of famous persons from history are becoming an increasing addition to the literature. While Lincoln may have had multiple endocrine neoplasia, there simply is no good evidence, clinical or historical, to believe he did. Good medicine requires more than photographs and neighborly descriptions to diagnose such serious diseases as Marfan syndrome and multiple endocrine neoplasia.

Blue Mass—Mercury Poisoning?

Consider a man in his fifties who has habitually ingested medical mercury; whose family and friends say that he demonstrates bizarre behavior and outbursts of rage, insomnia, and forgetfulness, whose hands are seen to tremble under stress, and who, after ceasing to take mercury because it made him "cross," behaves like a saint under the greatest personal and professional distress.[23]

Thus, three medical health professionals begin their article on Lincoln's abuse of "blue pills," questioning his diagnosed poisoning by ingesting elemental mercury for a period ranging from the late 1830s through the first month of his presidency in 1861, a period exceeding twenty-two years.

Mercury, in various forms, was commonly used for a variety of illnesses beginning in the early 1600s and reaching into the twentieth century. Its first use medicinally was for the treatment of syphilis. As time passed, its use spread to include such diseases or conditions as apoplexy (the bleeding into an organ or loss of blood flow to an organ, usually resulting in coma followed by death), tuberculosis, cholera, typhoid fever, and even to enhance fertility. By Lincoln's time, mercury was being prescribed for "melancholia" or depression, a malady Lincoln suffered from on occasion.

Poisoning can result from mercury vapor inhalation, ingestion, or absorption through the skin. The biological effects of mercury in the human body depend on the form to which the body is exposed. Ingestion of metallic mercury, such as Lincoln was suspected of doing, can lead to gastrointestinal irritation, inactivation of a wide variety of enzymes, and eventually to severe central nervous system damage. The degree of the damage is related to how much elemental mercury is converted to methyl mercury, the most serious form, and to its subsequent secretion through the kidneys and urine.

One of the common medicines prescribed in Lincoln's day for such maladies as constipation and depression (or hypochondriasis, also known as "the hypo") was a product known as "blue mass" or "blue pills." This drug was individually compounded by a druggist using mercury, and therefore it varied in composition and strength. The Lincolns were patrons of the Springfield druggists Corneau and

Diller. A search of their records show that Lincoln made 245 purchases, of which five were listed as "pills." No blue mass or blue pills are listed among any of the Lincoln purchases, but the five purchases of "pills" may have included the mercury-containing blue mass pills.[24] Even so, such a record is not consistent with long-term use of mercury pills. Ward Lamon, a Danville attorney and close friend of Lincoln, during an interview with William Herndon about Lincoln's behavior, said that Lincoln "took Blue pills—Blue Mass."[25] He didn't say how many, or for how long.

Whatever Lincoln's use, or non-use, of mercury drugs, there are recorded episodes of erratic or strange behavior on his part. Michael Burlingame, in his study *The Inner World of Abraham Lincoln*, writes of several incidents when Lincoln acted harshly, or in a belittling way toward others. Burlingame cites a close friend of Lincoln: "He was especially adept at cruel mimicry of accents, mannerisms, gestures, and physical defects."[26] He cites one particular incident involving the Grigsby brothers, Reuben and Charles, lampooning them in a satirical poem titled "The Chronicles of Reuben," where the two grooms were misled into switching bedrooms and brides on their wedding night.[27] While this may be an example of boorish behavior, it is not an example of neurological disorder. Lincoln's poem is not even an example of cruel behavior. It was meant to be—and was—humorous.

More to the point are examples of Lincoln's alleged episodes of rage or anger. At the time of his broken engagement to Mary Todd, his future sister-in-law, Elizabeth Todd Edwards, told William Herndon in an interview following Lincoln's death, "He loved Mary—he went crazy in my opinion—not because he loved Miss Edwards [Matilda] as Said, but because he wanted to marry and doubted his ability & Capacity to please and support a wife. . . . Mr. L failed to meet his Engagement—Cause insanity. In his lunacy he declared he hated Mary and loved Miss Edwards. This is true yet it was not his

Lincoln artist and scholar Lloyd Ostendorf painted an angry Lincoln for Elwell Crissey's book on Lincoln's Bloomington speech in 1856, *Lincoln's Lost Speech*. During his speech Lincoln became angry, shouting at the audience. Original art by Lloyd Ostendorf, used with permission.

real feelings. A Crazy man hates those he loves when not himself—often this is the case."[28]

Burlingame describes more serious behavior, quoting Lincoln's close friend Henry C. Whitney, who said Lincoln's face became "lurid with majestic and terrifying wrath," and another close friend, Isaac N. Arnold, who said, "his eyes would blaze with indignation, and his denunciation few could endure."[29] Lincoln also displayed signs of occasional memory loss and insomnia, both signs of mercury poisoning, but also signs of normal aging. Lincoln clearly did not suffer memory loss on a regular basis, which he would have if suffering from mercury poisoning.

Whatever Lincoln's habit of taking "blue pills" was, he eventually stopped the practice, telling his old law partner John T. Stuart that "they made him cross."[30] The examples of Lincoln's alleged erratic behavior may have been the result of his taking "blue pills" on occasion, or simply the behavior of a man passionately involved in life. In any event, neurological damage caused by mercury poisoning is not reversible. Stopping the ingestion of mercury does not result in the repair of whatever neurological damage may have occurred. This fact alone speaks against Lincoln's suffering mercury poisoning, at least to the extent of mental impairment as suggested by some to explain what may have been episodic moments of anger, rage, or forgetfulness.

The Hypo or Melancholia

Although he appeared to enjoy life rapturously, he was the victim of terrible melancholy . . . when by himself, he was so overcome with mental depression that he never dare carry a knife in his pocket.[31]

Robert Wilson

That Lincoln suffered from some form of depression is clear. No fewer than fourteen of his close associates, whose relationships with Lincoln spanned from the years of his youth in Indiana through his presidency, told of his constant battle with "melancholy." Their descriptions ranged from "sad" to "suicidal." Words like saddest, gloomiest, uncheery, impaired, and dejection were frequently used to describe Lincoln's moodiness.[32] But, in evaluating Lincoln's mental state of mind it is important to separate those periods associated with tragic or serious personal loses, such as the death of a loved one (his mother, his sister, Ann Rutledge, and his broken engagement to Mary

Todd), from everyday events that, while troublesome, would not cause a normal person to fall into deep despair. Too often all of the tragic events of Lincoln's life are lumped together with ordinary, nondepressive events.

Lincoln did suffer from a form of depression that went beyond the normal, but can it be considered "clinical depression"? Clinical depression (also called major depression) is characterized by the National Institute of Mental Health as "a combination of symptoms that interfere with a person's ability to work, sleep, study, eat, and enjoy once-pleasurable activities." Clinical depression often goes hand in hand with bipolar disorder, which the NIMH defines as "mental disorder marked by extreme changes in mood, thought, energy and behavior."[33]

While it seems clear that Lincoln suffered from occasional mood swings similar to bipolar behavior, he was not clinically depressed, nor was he truly bipolar. At no time during his professional career was he continuously plagued by an inability to work, sleep, study, or eat, and while he showed signs of mood swings (don't we all), they did not reach the clinical definition of depression. The key words here are "continuous" and "clinical depression."

The Lincoln literature is replete with examples of Lincoln's depression. Michael Burlingame gives us numerous examples in his interesting account *The Inner World of Abraham Lincoln*.[34] One particular incident related in his book is the recollection of Lincoln's legal colleague and friend Henry C. Whitney. During the 1850 session of the Eighth Circuit, Whitney, while sharing a bed with Lincoln, was awakened when Lincoln sat up in bed "talking the weirdest and most incoherent nonsense all to himself. . . . After at least five minutes of weird gabbling, Lincoln jumped up, hurriedly washed and dressed, then stoked the fire, before which he sat moodily, dejectedly, in a most somber and gloomy spell." Whitney goes on to point out that Lincoln "emerged from his cave of gloom and came back . . . to the world in which he lived again."[35] Whitney's description of Lincoln's behavior, while odd, is not clinical depression. Lincoln quickly recovered.

The fact that Lincoln "came back to the world in which he lived" is too sudden a mood shift to be an example of true depression. Even so, Lincoln's behavior was atypical at times. Everyone who knew Lincoln on a personal basis recognized his peculiar behavior, describing it as melancholy. Whitney seems to be the clearest witness to Lincoln's melancholy. Whitney saw Lincoln perform in court, where his mood swings were never apparent, except for the occasional show of anger when he felt misquoted. In one court incident Herndon described Lincoln as becoming "wrought up to the point of madness."[36] Another instance where Lincoln "erupted in anger" involved a former political ally and fellow lawyer who supported Stephen Douglas in the 1858 senatorial campaign.[37]

It is interesting that these episodes of "un-Lincoln-like" behavior are attributed to mercury poisoning by Norbert Hirschhorn on the one hand, and to bipolar behavior on the other. It seems that in every instance where Lincoln transgressed his saint-like image he rebounded to form. This is not the result one finds in the clinically depressed or those suffering bipolar disorder or mercury poisoning.

Syphilis

A little over fifty years ago I gave a talk on Lincoln's assassination to a Civil War Round Table consisting almost entirely of neo-Confederate members, most of whom were Sons of Confederate Veterans. When I finished my talk, the first question was really a rhetorical statement. Was it not true, the questioner asked, that Lincoln had contracted syphilis as a young man and given it to his wife, Mary, thereby driving her insane? Couldn't it also be true, I answered somewhat facetiously, that it was Mary who contracted syphilis and gave it to Lincoln, thereby accounting for his "erratic behavior"?

The Ailing Lincoln

It seems odd to speak of syphilis and Abraham Lincoln in the same context, but, like everything else about Lincoln, it occasionally rears its ugly head. Ugly because the charge that Lincoln contracted syphilis, if true, denigrates his image in modern eyes. You will not find the subject of syphilis in the great majority of Lincoln biographies, or even in the few books discussing his health problems. The most thorough and accurate discussion in the literature is in volume 1 of Michael Burlingame's *Abraham Lincoln: A Life*. Burlingame cites an interview of Joshua Speed, Lincoln's best friend and confidant in his youth, by William Herndon. Speed had a reputation of frequenting prostitutes—or at the very least visiting one or two women for sex—while living in Springfield. The salient parts are worth reproducing here:

> Speed said that around 1839 or 1840 [Lincoln was living in Springfield at the time], "he was keeping a pretty woman" in Springfield and Lincoln "desirous, to have *a little*" asked his bunkmate, "do you know where I can get *some*." Speed replied, "Yes I do, & if you will wait a moment or so I'll send you to the place with a note. You can't get it without a note or by my appearance." Armed with the note from Speed, Lincoln went to see the girl—handed her the note after a short "how do you do etc." Lincoln told his business and the girl, after some protestations, agreed to satisfy him. Things went on right—Lincoln and the girl stript off and went to bed. Before anything was done Lincoln said to the girl "How much do you charge?" "Five dollars, Mr. Lincoln," Mr. Lincoln said, "I've only got $3." Well said the girl, "I'll trust you, Mr. Lincoln, for $2." Lincoln thought a moment or so and said—"I do not wish to go on credit—I'm poor & I don't know where my next dollar will come from and I cannot afford to Cheat you." Lincoln after some words of encouragement from the girl got up out of bed—buttoned up his pants and offered the girl the $3.00, which she would not take saying—Mr. Lincoln—"you are the most Conscientious man I ever saw." Lincoln went out of the house, bidding the girl good

141

evening and went to the store of Speed saying nothing. Speed asked no questions and so the matter rested a day or so. Speed had occasion to go and see the girl in a few days, and she told him just what was said and done between herself & Lincoln and Speed told me the story and I have no doubt of its truthfulness.[38]

Of course, such a visit would not result in Lincoln catching a sexually transmitted disease since nothing happened in the way of sex. Lincoln may have tried again, but no record exists to support such a claim. Rumors existed, perhaps in jest, that Lincoln was the father of two children with two different women in New Salem, both married to friends of Lincoln. It is simply not plausible that Lincoln would have intercourse with the wives of two of his best New Salem friends. The rumors were meant to tease Lincoln.

An interesting side note concerns Joshua Speed and his paramour. While it appears Speed frequented the young woman for sex, there is no evidence that he ever contracted syphilis. He showed no signs of the disease through his later life. Herndon often remarked that Lincoln had a strong attraction to beautiful women, but also remarked that he was faithful to his wife, Mary, throughout their marriage.

Smallpox or Variola

Smallpox is a highly infectious disease caused by a virus that is often fatal. There are two forms of the disease, caused by two variants of the virus, Variola major and Variola minor. The first is the more serious and proves fatal in about 30 percent of cases, while the second is far less dangerous, with a death rate of only 1 percent.

Smallpox is believed to have existed as early as ten thousand years ago, and positive traces of the disease have been found in Egyptian mummies dating from 3,000 B.C. In the twentieth century, smallpox was responsible for 300 million deaths and one-third of the world's blindness. Since the development of a vaccine in 1798 by British scientist Edward Jenner, intensified efforts through vaccination have eradicated the major form of the disease. The last known case of smallpox occurred in 1977, and the disease was officially declared eradicated by the World Health Organization in 1980. Its eradication was one of the truly great triumphs of modern medicine.

While in Gettysburg to deliver his famous Gettysburg Address on November 19, 1863, Lincoln contracted the milder Variola form of the disease. He spent the return trip to Washington in a makeshift bed aboard the military train that carried him home. Lincoln spent the next two weeks recovering from the disease and quipped to his two young secretaries, "Now I have something I can give to everybody."[39] Lincoln was fortunate. He may well have developed a level of natural immunity in his youth that limited the effect of the disease in his case.

Vaccination existed within the Union army, and numerous soldiers were vaccinated early in the war. Of the 364,000 soldiers who would die of infectious disease during the war, Variola major would kill only 7,000.[40] Still, the disease ranked fifth among the diseases that devastated the Union army, dysentery being the number one killer of Union soldiers.

The Milk Sick or Brucellosis?

In the first part of the nineteenth century most causes of death were little understood, or not understood at all. The sudden onset of illness that ended in death was the result of "visitations," or "providence." The "night air" could invade the normally healthy bodies of men, women, and children and snuff life from them. Young Ann Rutledge died in the prime of life from "brain fever" brought on by the stress of her having been engaged to two men at the same time, or so people believed at the time. She may well have died of typhoid fever, a common killer in the nineteenth century. Disease was shrouded in mystery, but, as one observer wrote, "it is doubtful if one was ever more shrouded in mystery than milk sickness."[41] And it just might be true that it is still shrouded in mystery today.

While Abraham Lincoln did not personally suffer from a disease known in the nineteenth century as "the milk sick," or "milk sickness," the disease figured prominently in his life, killing his mother while he was "in his tenth year." The death of Nancy Hanks Lincoln was the first major tragedy experienced by Lincoln, and undoubtedly had a significant effect on his mental well-being. While his father remarried a year later to a woman who became a loving stepmother to the young boy and his sister, the loss of his mother at such a young age surely affected him.

Milk sickness is believed to be caused by a chemical compound known as tremetone found in the milk and meat of infected cows. The chemical substance is found in the snakeroot plant (*Ageratina altissima*),[42] which can be found growing in the rich, shaded woodlands of West Virginia, Ohio, Indiana, Illinois, Kentucky, and Tennessee. The plant is indigenous to the United States and was unknown to European settlers, who first encountered its effects along the early western frontier.

The causative agent was originally known as tremetol, but tremetol proved to be a mixture of organic compounds, one of which was tremetone, the actual agent that is believed to cause the disease. Tremetone is defined medically as an unsaturated alcohol obtained from the plant genus *Ageratina* that causes trembles (shaking) in cattle and sheep, and similar symptoms in humans.[43] It is a neurotoxin. Neurotoxins are substances that act on the nervous system. Typical symptoms are weakness in the limbs, headache, vision loss, loss of memory, trembling, vomiting, and loss of cognitive function. The illness is thought to come from drinking the milk or eating the

Blossoms of the white snakeroot plant (*Ageratina altissima*). Wikimedia Commons, photograph by Daina Krummins.

meat of cattle that have ingested the plant known commonly as snakeroot.

Milk sickness, often called puking fever or trembles, is believed to be caused by the ingested tremetone's interfering with normal metabolic processes, resulting in what is medically referred to as severe ketosis and associated acidosis. In many ways it resembles the crisis found in type 1 diabetes in which dangerously high levels of blood sugar result in lowering the pH of the blood, adversely affecting the liver and kidneys. Unchecked production of fatty acid metabolism will lead to increased levels of ketones and high levels of glucose in the blood, resulting in ketoacidosis, and kidney and liver damage.[44] The peculiar odor of a stricken person's breath is due to the high levels of ketones in their bloodstream.

In 1818, two years after Thomas Lincoln settled his family in Indiana near Little Pigeon Creek, his wife, Nancy, came down with the illness. There was no treatment, and the result was fatal. Shortly prior to Nancy Hanks Lincoln's death she had attended to her close neighbors, Thomas and Elizabeth Sparrow, and Mrs. Peter Brooner. All three were suffering from milk sickness and would die. Although milk sickness is not contagious, Nancy would fall ill with the same disease one week after the Sparrows' deaths.

At the time the fatal illness struck the Indiana community, Dennis Hanks, Nancy Hanks Lincoln's cousin, then nineteen years old, was living in the home of Elizabeth and Thomas Sparrow. Living in the Thomas Lincoln home at the same time were Sarah and Abraham Lincoln, eleven and nine years old respectively. The fact that these three young people escaped the disease, although presumably consuming daily amounts of tainted milk, is puzzling. The same can be said for the other numerous people consuming tainted cow's milk in the area. Chemical poisoning by a neurotoxin such as tremetone is not selective. Consuming the poison results in symptoms, and almost always death. The fact that some people succumb to the disease while others in the same household do not is suggestive of infectious disease, not chemical poisoning.

Is it possible that the real cause of death could be the bacterium *Brucella*? Brucellosis is an infectious disease caused by the bacterium *Brucella melitennsis,* and it is transmitted through the milk of cows and their meat. The symptoms are similar to those described for Nancy Hanks Lincoln: fever, malaise, vomiting, and headache, all lasting two to three weeks.

The possibility of Nancy Hanks Lincoln's sickness being an infectious disease rather than a metabolic disease is suggested by the fact that neither of the Lincoln children, who presumably drank the

146

same milk as their mother, contracted the disease. Infectious diseases vary in their victims; not everyone exposed to the bacterium succumbs to its effects. The predominant symptom is fever, often accompanied by chills, sweats, and weakness. Other symptoms may include fatigue, headache, weight loss, and severe joint pain. This description rather neatly fits the symptoms described by Dennis Hanks and others for victims of the milk sickness.

In his authoritative biography of Abraham Lincoln, titled *Lincoln*, historian David Donald wrote, "Then the Pigeon Creek community was devastated by an attack of what was called milk sickness (more properly, *brucellosis*)." When queried as to his source for this statement by the author, Donald responded, "I believe that I rested my statement on an article in the *Indiana Magazine of History*, but I alone am to blame for the slip. . . . It has been corrected in the Touchstone paperback edition of the book."[45] Perhaps Professor Donald reacted to his critics too quickly. He may well have been correct in citing brucellosis as the real agent behind the milk sick. Nevertheless, it is an interesting thought.

Lincoln appeared different to different people in differing circumstances. He was both private and public, thoughtful and cruel, calm and angry, tolerant and intolerant, patient and impatient. It is not difficult to build Lincoln's character in varying forms. There is a wealth of material to draw from. It is said that there are over eighteen thousand publications on Lincoln, second only to Jesus Christ. One can find book-length accounts of Lincoln on everything from women to sex to finances to railroads. An author can choose which Lincoln he wishes to create, and find ample material to bolster his or her case. To some, Lincoln may have had Marfan syndrome, experienced clinical depression, suffered from mercury poisoning, been infected with syphilis, or had multiple endocrine neoplasia, not to mention flat feet, but there is no reliable evidence that he was worse off health-wise than those he grew up and lived with. He is a man whose stature in history is so great that every little aspect of his life has been picked at by hundreds of historians (and nonhistorians), and justifiably so. He is truly a man for all seasons.

The Longevity of the Lincoln Lineage

One measure of good health, particularly in the nineteenth century, is longevity. Diseases such as Marfan, MEN 2b, and mercury poisoning seriously limit one's life expectancy, especially if the individual has all three, as claimed for Lincoln. Lincoln was the seventh generation of his family in North America. His great-great-great-great-grandfather Samuel Lincoln immigrated to North America in 1637 from England and died at the age of seventy-one from natural causes. Samuel's son and grandson, Mordecai and Mordecai II, lived to the ages of seventy and fifty, respectively. Lincoln's great-grandfather and grandfather, John and Abraham, lived to the ages of seventy-two and forty-two, but Abraham was killed by an Indian ambush while tilling his fields. Lincoln's father lived to be seventy-three. His mother died prematurely of disease at the age of thirty-four. Longevity was also found in Abraham Lincoln's collateral ancestors, many living into their seventies. Omitting the grandfather who was murdered, the average age at death for the Lincoln lineage was sixty-seven, well advanced for the period of history in which they lived.

Longevity was not the only trait of the Lincoln lineage. Success was also a common feature. Going as far back as the early 1500s in England through the 1800s in America, the Lincolns prospered financially. Land owners, weavers, iron makers, farmers—the Lincolns were among the upper class of their communities. Prolific in creating families, they were also prolific in accumulating wealth. Many of the Lincoln homesteads still exist, attesting to their wealth. Richard Lincoln's elegant brick home, built in the early 1500s, still stands in Swanton Morley, England, now a local pub. The homes of

Samuel Lincoln, his son Mordecai, and grandson Mordecai II are elegant private homes in Massachusetts and Pennsylvania. The farms of Virginia John Lincoln, Captain Abraham Lincoln, and Thomas Lincoln are still in tillage, growing crops years after their original owners passed away.

Abraham Lincoln was the recipient of a special combination of genes passed down over centuries from his Anglo-Saxon forebears. There appears to be a strain of hardiness and intellect that placed the Lincolns among the firsts of their generations. Intellect is a part of health, and Lincoln's intellect was unsurpassed by his fellow countrymen both before and after his brief life.

London Punch editorial cartoon mocking Britain's dependence on Southern cotton and noting its being more important than British wool. *London Punch*, 1862. Library of Congress.

Mr. Lincoln dismisses John Bull. England offered Lincoln a $15 million loan based on American cotton as security, but found no takers. In the cartoon Lincoln rejects the offer while leaning against a fifteen-inch cannon, saying, "Good morning, John." *Harper's Weekly*, May 16, 1863.

8 Trading with the Enemy

> By allowing trading with the South in contradiction of his own laws, [Lincoln] enriched a circle of powerful people who, once he had outlived his usefulness and handed over the arrangements to others, marked himself very quickly for assassination.
>
> Charles Higham, *Murdering Mr. Lincoln*

The above claim, like most Lincoln conspiratorial claims, is an attempt to sensationalize the president's assassination by mixing fact with fiction. It is bad history. By treating a little-known event in history, some authors are able to manipulate the uninformed—a practice many historians refer to as "shock history." It reflects a growing trend in the revisionist lure that is becoming prevalent in modern historical writing.

It is true that among the lesser-known practices that occurred during the Civil War was a carefully crafted policy promoting trade between Northern agents and members of the Confederacy. The policy was riddled with corruption, and dozens of Northern Republicans were becoming millionaires. When Lincoln decided to end the practice, modern conspiracy theorists conclude, members of Lincoln's own party plotted to remove him from office so that the deals could continue to go through. That the policy was illegal, as claimed by authors like Higham, and that it resulted in Lincoln's assassination are without any foundation in fact.

The policy was aimed at preventing Southern cotton from reaching England and France and providing the Confederacy with much needed gold, and weapons, and at supplying Northern mills with much-needed cotton, keeping the Northern textile trade in business. In addition, the government required that 25 percent of all revenues from the sale of cotton purchased by Northern agents be paid to the US Treasury, thereby helping to offset the enormous cost of the war. This little-known program has given rise to claims of widespread corruption and treason, resulting in Lincoln's assassination.[1] The Congress, it turns out, had given Lincoln and the US Treasury Department the authority to issue permits to trade with the enemy in territory occupied by the Union military.[2]

The unusual policy had its origin in Lincoln's naval blockade of Southern ports. Not only did the blockade cut off the South's importation of essential goods, but it also greatly reduced the export of cotton to European markets.[3] On April 16, just four days after the firing on Fort Sumter, Lincoln issued a proclamation ordering a naval blockade of the ports within those states in rebellion in an attempt to prevent any commerce from taking place. Four months later, on August 16, 1861, Lincoln issued a second proclamation banning all "commercial intercourse between inhabitants of those states in rebellion." Lincoln's proclamation stated that "all goods and chattels, wares and merchandize" coming from rebellious states be seized by the United States.[4]

The blockade, together with the ban on commercial intercourse with the South, resulted in a severe shortage of most goods that had been a part of Southern life. Most affected was cotton. Cotton was the lifeblood of the Confederacy, accounting for nearly 70 percent of the South's income (it represented 59 percent of the nation's exports).[5] It was also essential to the economies of Britain and France. Prior to the war, Southern cotton accounted for 78 percent of the cotton used by British mills and 90 percent of the cotton consumed by French mills.[6]

By 1860, cotton sales brought over $100 million in sales to the South. Shortly before the war began, James Hammond of South Carolina proclaimed, "Old England would topple headlong and carry the whole civilized world with her. No, you dare not make war on cotton. Cotton is king."[7] It was this dependency on Southern cotton that led the Southern leaders to believe that Britain and France would support the Confederacy and come to recognize it as an independent nation. Interestingly, to force recognition, the South placed a temporary ban on exporting cotton to Europe. The shortage of cotton in European mills would surely bring Britain and France to recognize the Confederacy.[8] England, however, had anticipated just such a ban and had stockpiled enough cotton to keep some of her mills operating. When the ban failed to bring the two nations to the South's side, the Confederacy lifted the ban and began trying to run cotton through the naval blockade.[9]

Lincoln's blockade was so successful that the equivalent of only one-eighth of the cotton exported prior to the war reached England.[10] As a result, the price of cotton increased eightfold, meaning the Confederacy realized as much profit from the sale of exported cotton during the war as it did before the blockade. This meant, as Lincoln pointed out, the South needed only one-eighth the labor and one-eighth of the land to produce the cotton, thereby freeing up labor to support the Confederate war effort, and land for raising other crops essential to sustain the South and her armies.

To relieve the situation, Lincoln decided to allow limited commerce with Southern cotton growers under controlled conditions. When Lincoln banned all commercial intercourse with the South, he exempted those parts that were occupied by Union forces, such as Norfolk, Memphis, and New Orleans. As a part of this exemption the Treasury Department was authorized to issue special permits to certain loyal citizens allowing them to trade with the enemy. The reasoning behind this policy was twofold: first, to encourage Southern Unionists, of whom Lincoln believed there were many, to send their cotton north, thereby supporting the Northern textile industry, and second, to prevent the cotton from slipping through the blockade and aiding the enemy. Lincoln believed that Southerners benefitted more from shipping through the blockade than trading with Northern dealers. His one stipulation was to ban purchasing cotton with gold. All purchases had to be made with Union "greenbacks."[11] Gold in the hands of the Confederacy was more dangerous to the Union cause than guns. With gold the Confederacy could strengthen its economy and literally buy anything, including ships built in British shipyards.

Lincoln's policy of allowing trade with Southern cotton growers was strongly opposed by most of the military. Both Grant and Sherman opposed the policy and made their feelings known to Secretary of War Edwin Stanton and Lincoln. Initially, Lincoln was undeterred. He told a protesting General Edward Canby, "Better give him guns for it than let him, as now, get both guns and ammunition."[12] It was a specious argument, for with the money raised from selling cotton the South was still able to purchase guns and ammunition.

Charles Gould, of New York, illustrates the lucrative math of trading profits.[13] Traders holding Treasury permits could purchase a standard 400-pound bale of captured cotton for $100 in greenbacks, which they could sell in New York for $500. The government was entitled to one-fourth the sale price, leaving the seller with $375. The trader was allowed to take one-third of the profit, or $125, back to the Confederacy in material goods, which he could sell to Southern buyers. For $125 the trader could purchase 568 pounds of bacon at 22 cents a pound and sell it to Southern buyers at $6 a pound, or $3,408 (in Confederate money). With the $3,408 in Confederate currency the trader could now buy 2,180 pounds of cotton (roughly five bales) at $1.25 a pound. But the Confederacy gave a 20 percent discount, so the actual cost to the buyer was just $2,726. Selling the 2,180 pounds

Ulysses S. Grant. Edward
Steers Jr. collection.

Secretary of War Edwin M.
Stanton. General Grant opposed Lincoln's trade policy, and convinced Secre-
tary Stanton to persuade
Lincoln to modify the policy within Grant's area of
control. Edward Steers Jr.
collection.

of cotton in New York would net the seller $2,045 after paying the US Treasury its 25 percent duty. Through such trading of cotton for bacon, an authorized trader would see his initial $100 investment realize just over $2,000, quite a handsome profit.

Robert Lamon, the brother of Lincoln's close friend and Danville, Illinois, law partner, received three permits totaling 50,000 bales. Leonard Swett, another political friend of Lincoln, together with several associates, received three permits to bring out 150,000 bales.[14] These permits resulted in profits totaling in the millions. Such profits created a rush of speculators and enterprising traders. Needless to say, the cotton trading business soon deteriorated into an unseemly and unhealthy business of graft and corruption, leading people like Grant, Sherman, and Stanton to oppose the practice. Even so, Lincoln continued the issuance of cotton permits up to the day of his death, except in certain areas under the control of Grant's armies. While a few Union army officers resigned their commissions so they might engage in the trading practice, most of the army's commanding generals opposed the trade policy and urged Lincoln to end it.[15]

Grant eventually prevailed on Secretary of War Stanton to get the president to cease the trading practice, as Grant believed it impeded the war effort. Lincoln acquiesced and authorized Grant to suspend all Treasury permits southeast of the Appalachian Mountains, but he allowed the trading to continue in other parts of the Confederacy, which included Texas, Louisiana, Mississippi, and Alabama. Grant then issued orders to his subordinates to seize all of the cotton under permits and hold it for "the benefit of the government."[16] According to certain conspiracy theorists, transferring authority to Grant and allowing him to shut down the cotton trade east of the Appalachian Mountains set the stage for Lincoln's assassination.[17]

With the fall of New Orleans, Memphis, and Norfolk, trading cotton through these cities northward became rather easy. Even so, trading became increasingly risky financially as the war headed toward its final months. From a high of $1.90 a pound in early 1864, cotton fell to $1.41 in November, to 85 cents in February, and to 40 cents in April following Lee's surrender. Cotton traders were taking increasing risks as the price plummeted, and several lost heavily in the end.[18]

With the end of the war, cotton trading using the permit policy came to an end. Of course, cotton continued to be in great demand, and Northerners worked closely with Southerners to locate and take cotton North. Lincoln's trade policy, while fostering a certain amount of corruption, in the end helped bolster the North's finances and weaken the South's. It had the added benefit of enticing certain Southerners to back the Union if for no other reason than greed. Dealing with the Union enemy could be lucrative for Southerners as well as Northerners. The negative aspects of the trade policy, such as providing the Confederacy and its armies with much needed food and money, worked against hastening the end of the war. William C. Harris, in his book *Lincoln's Last Months,* chastised Lincoln for not taking a closer hold over the questionable practice of trading with the enemy. He wrote, "Lincoln did not demonstrate the kind of close attention and able leadership that he gave to winning the war, ending slavery, and restoring the South to the Union. . . . He could have done better."[19]

Trading with the enemy has fueled conspiracy theorists such as Higham, Leonard Guttridge, and Ray Neff into claiming that Lincoln's closing down the practice in certain areas led to his murder.[20] As historian Harris writes, "Because Orville Browning, Leonard Swett, and Ward Hill Lamon, all close friends of Lincoln, benefited from the trade does not mean that they wanted Lincoln dead after he gave General Grant the authority to close the commerce through his lines."[21]

These conspiracy theorists believe the trade was illegal and those who engaged in it were traitors.[22] It was, in fact, legal. Because of the money involved, it became more of a patronage scandal involving greed rather than treasonous activity. While unseemly, it was legal in every aspect. Both Lincoln and the US Congress approved the trade and tried to regulate it, albeit with marginal success.

Lincoln's motives were good, and his approval of trading with the enemy was meant to help the Union far more than it helped the Confederacy. It raised money to finance the war, provided desperately needed cotton to New England mills (which helped in Lincoln's reelection in 1864), and helped keep Britain and France from recognizing the Confederacy by keeping cotton flowing to their mills, though at lower volumes than before the war.

While some twentieth-century historians looked on the practice unfavorably, and some even considered it "treasonable,"[23] it was justified in its conception, if not in its practice. While many of Lincoln's friends profited from trading for cotton, Lincoln did not benefit personally, although he could have. In the end, trading with the enemy proved to be a controversial policy both during the war and in the eyes of many modern-day historians. When General Edward R. S. Canby protested vigorously against the policy because greed had taken over much of the trade, Lincoln responded by telling Canby, "If pecuniary greed can be made to aid us in such an effort, let us be thankful that so much good can be got out of pecuniary greed."[24] Ever the pragmatist, Lincoln believed his policy of "trading with the enemy" proved beneficial to the Union's war efforts.

9 West Virginia

Abraham Lincoln's Illegitimate Child

> The subsequent organization of the state of West Virginia
> and its separation from the state of Virginia were acts
> of secession. Thus we have insurrection, revolution, and
> secession.
>
> Jefferson Davis

The irony of Jefferson Davis's statement is self-evident. The great secessionist found the secession of western Virginia from the rest of Virginia to be insurrection and revolution. Clearly, the chickens had come home to roost. Abraham Lincoln, following his signing of the bill admitting West Virginia as the thirty-fifth state to join the Union, put Davis's words into perspective, writing, "It is said that the admission of West Virginia is secession, and tolerated only because it is our secession. Well, if we call it by that name, there is still difference enough between secession against the constitution and secession in favor of the constitution."[1] It was, Lincoln said, "expedient."

Ironically, West Virginia entered the Union as a slave state at the very moment the Union was fighting to end slavery. Because it was loyal to the Union, it was exempt from the effects of the Emancipation Proclamation. The event was marked by considerable controversy from several quarters, both North and South, including from members of President Lincoln's own cabinet. The legality of the admission of West Virginia is still debated among historians and constitutional scholars, and the state is frequently referred to as "Abraham Lincoln's illegitimate child." Was the formation of West Virgin-

Abraham Lincoln Walks at Midnight. The statue by West Virginia sculptor Fred Martin Torrey is inspired by the poem "Abraham Lincoln Walks at Midnight" by Springfield, Illinois, poet Vachel Lindsey. It stands in front of West Virginia's capitol building. Photograph by Todd Carpenter.

ia legal according to the US Constitution, or was it simply an act of usurpation by Lincoln, proving that might makes right?

According to the US Constitution, Article IV, Section 3:

> New states may be admitted by the Congress into this union; but no new state shall be formed or erected within the jurisdiction of any other state; nor any state be formed by the junction of two or more states, or parts of states, without the consent of the legislatures of the states concerned as well as of the Congress.

The last part of Section 3 plainly states: "without the consent of the legislatures of the states concerned. . . ." And yet, in 1863, fifty of Virginia's counties west of the Blue Ridge Mountains seceded from that state and formed a new state. Jefferson Davis opined, "Will any intelligent person assert that the consent of the state of Virginia was given to the formation of this new state?"[2] The problem, of course, was that Virginia, along with its state legislature and officers, seceded

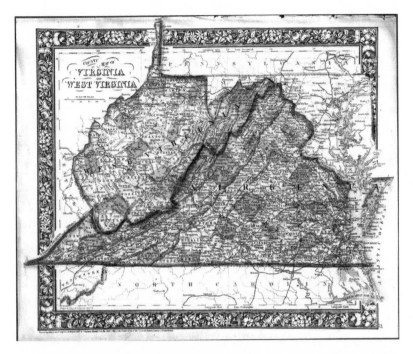

The states of Virginia and West Virginia following the formation of West Virginia in 1863. Augustus Mitchell Jr., cartographer, 1863.

from the Union in April 1861 to join the newly formed Confederate States of America. Virginia would never agree to such a dismemberment under any circumstances, including her own secession from the Union. How was this seemingly impossible maneuver of creating a new state accomplished, and did it satisfy the constitutional requirement spelled out in Article IV, Section 3?

The reasons that the western counties of Virginia (the Allegheny Mountains region) wanted to remain in the Union, and therefore secede from Virginia, are complex and go back several decades prior to the Civil War.[3] Treated over the years as the Tidewater's stepchild, the western counties were constantly forced to give up much to the Tidewater area, getting little in return. Constituting two-fifths of the land, and one-fourth of the population, the western counties felt constantly ignored by the Tidewater-dominated legislature of Virginia.

At the start of the Civil War, Virginia's population totaled 1,291,641, of whom 472,494 were slaves. Of these figures, the western counties had a population of 376,677 (29 percent of the total population), of whom 18,371 (only 5 percent) were slaves. The US Constitution provided for purposes of determining representation in state and national legislatures the number of free persons, plus "three-fifths of all other persons." The "three-fifths" were slaves who, although considered noncitizens, were added to the final count. This provision of the Constitution meant that the area outside the western counties added 273,673 persons to its total population count while the western counties were credited with only 11,000 additional persons. Because of the three-fifths provision of the Constitution, the western counties suffered a disproportionately lower representation in the Virginia state legislature (and the US House of Representatives). Therefore, when it came to voting on various pieces of legislation, the western counties were at a significant disadvantage, resulting in a growing animosity toward the Piedmont and Tidewater regions of the state.

In February 1861, Virginia delegates met in Richmond to decide the question of secession. After weeks of debate, delegates finally voted on April 17, 1861, in favor of secession, 88 to 55. Of the 55 votes against secession, 42 were delegates from the western counties. Determined to remain loyal to the Union, certain individuals in the western counties saw their chance to disassociate themselves from the rest of Virginia, an idea that had been growing within the region for several years. Two major events followed Virginia's secession. The first was the formation of a new Virginia government loyal to the Union. The second event was the formation of a new state carved from Virginia's western counties. Both of these events brought about a bitter controversy between the two regions.

Following the adoption of the secession ordinance by the Richmond convention, the western delegates returned home and called for their own convention to decide what steps to take in protecting their own interests. Twelve hundred people met in a hastily called convention in the city of Clarksburg, the birthplace of Stonewall Jackson. It was decided that each western county would select delegates and meet in convention in the city of Wheeling on May 13 in what would become known as the First Wheeling Convention. When the convention began, 436 delegates from twenty-seven counties were in attendance. The purpose of the convention was to decide just what to do about the state's plan to secede from the Union. While some of the delegates pushed for immediate secession from Virginia, cooler heads decided to wait and meet at a second convention following the statewide referendum on the question of secession.[4]

On May 23, the vote total from the Tidewater and Piedmont counties came to 122,716 votes for secession, 8,412 against. The votes from the western counties were not included. Officials claimed that conditions prevented the western votes from reaching Richmond in time. Governor John Letcher estimated the missing votes at 3,234 for secession and 11,961 against, bringing the final statewide vote to 125,950 for, 20,373 against. Letcher greatly misrepresented the western counties' votes, which came in at 19,121 for secession, 34,677 against. Those figures would have brought the true vote statewide to 141,837 for secession, and 43,089 against. Letcher's ratio of 6 to 1 in favor of succession was actually closer to 3 to 1. Once again, the western counties were shortchanged by the political operatives in Richmond.[5]

Those 34,677 votes cast in the western counties against secession were a powerful force. With Virginia's secession a reality, the Second Wheeling Convention met in June and declared the Virginia Convention illegal since it convened without the necessary referendum required by the Virginia state constitution. Since the convention was declared illegal, the ordinance of secession was declared illegal, and all state offices occupied by secessionists were declared vacant. The western delegates would create a new state government loyal to the Union. They would elect a new governor and two new senators, replacing those who had seceded to join the Confederacy. It was a bold move.

The Wheeling Convention passed an ordinance establishing a new "Restored Government of Virginia." The delegates elected a new governor and two new senators to replace the Senate seats vacated by Virginia's two senators that resigned from the US Senate and joined the Confederacy. The three members of the US House of Representatives retained their House seats since they had remained loyal to the Union. But was the newly created government legal? Virginia had two governments, one in secession, the other created by what some considered a rogue government. What are the rules that determine the legitimate government of a state, and, importantly, who decides which government is the lawful government?

The question of who legally represents a state was settled by the Supreme Court in an interesting case in 1849, fourteen years before the formation of West Virginia. The ruling came in a little-known court case titled *Luther v. Borden*.[6] The state of Rhode Island lacked a state constitution. It operated under a Royal Charter granted by King Charles II of England in 1663 to the Colony of Rhode Island that allowed settlers there to govern themselves. One of the provisions of the charter restricted voting rights to white males twenty-one years and older who owned a minimum of $150 in property. This provision excluded large numbers of males, who decided to take matters into their own hands.

In 1840, Thomas Wilson Dorr, a former state legislator, formed a new party, "The People's Party." A convention was held, a state constitution was drafted granting suffrage to all white males twenty-one

Thomas Wilson Dorr.
Edward Steers Jr.
collection.

and older with a minimum of one year's residence, and Dorr was elected governor. In 1842, the existing state government and the "Dorrites," as they were now called, held elections, resulting in two governments headed by two governors. Samuel Ward King, the governor under the old system, known as "Charterites," declared martial law. The Dorrites (The People's Party) attempted to seize the state arsenal but failed. Dorr fled to New York only to later return to Rhode Island, where he was found guilty of treason and sentenced to life in prison. He was released after serving fewer than three years.

Although the rebellion failed, it eventually led to a republican form of government under a new state constitution in keeping with the guarantees of the US Constitution. The rebellion generated an interesting court case in which the US Supreme Court handed down a ruling spelling out which government was the lawful government of a state. This ruling directly affected the authority of the "Restored Government of Virginia."

One of the Dorrites, Martin Luther, brought suit in federal court claiming the old government was not a "republican form of government" as guaranteed by the US Constitution. Luther maintained in his lawsuit that the charter government was not a "republican" government because it restricted the electorate to only the most propertied classes. Article IV, Section 4, of the US Constitution states, "The United States shall guarantee to every State in this Union a Republican Form of Government."[7] Luther argued that the Supreme Court should find that the Dorrite government was the lawful Republican government of Rhode Island.

In 1849 the Supreme Court, headed by Chief Justice Roger Brooke Taney, ruled that the question before the court was not a legal question, but a political question to be decided by the Congress of the United States and the president. The legislators that Congress voted to seat in the Senate and the House would represent the legal government of that state. They added that whoever the president recognized as governor also determines the government of that state.[8]

A little over a decade later, after some debate, the US Senate seated the newly elected senators. Since the Virginia Senate seats were vacant when the Senate met, it agreed to seat both new senators representing the Restored Government, Thomas Waitman Willey and John S. Carlile, thereby satisfying the Supreme Court's ruling in *Luther v. Borden*. Lincoln, in various correspondences with Francis Pierpont, the newly elected governor of the Restored Government, accepted Pierpont as the political head of that government, thereby satisfying the Court's ruling concerning presidential recognition. Virginia had a new government loyal to the Union.[9]

Having sanctioned the newly formed government of Virginia, the western counties quickly petitioned the new legislature for permission to form a new state. The delegates of the Second Wheeling Convention reconvened on August 6, 1862, and drafted a resolution

Thomas Waitman Willey.
Library of Congress.

John S. Carlile. Library of
Congress.

calling for a public referendum on the question of statehood to be held on October 24. Of those citizens voting, the referendum passed overwhelmingly 18,408 to 781. With the people's approval, albeit limited in number, the delegates met again to draw the boundaries of the new state and adopt a name. After considerable debate, the fifty westernmost counties (all lying within the Allegheny Mountains) were selected along with the name "West Virginia."[10] A constitution was drafted and submitted to a second referendum, with 18,862 voting for and 514 voting against ratification.

Having established the boundaries of the new state and adopted a publicly approved constitution, the Restored Government of Virginia was asked for permission to establish the new state from the existing counties of Virginia. Remember, the US Constitution under Article IV, Section 3, stated that new states may be admitted into this Union, but only with the consent of the state concerned as well as the consent of the Congress.

The newly formed legislature of the Restored Government of Virginia gave its approval for creation of the new state. This assumed that the Restored Government was the legitimate government of Virginia. Assuming it was, only one more hurdle remained before statehood for West Virginia became official: approval by the US Congress. With the approval in hand, Waitman Willey, one of the two senators representing the Restored Government of Virginia, introduced a bill into the Senate calling for Congress to approve statehood for West Virginia. The Senate approved the bill, sending it to the House of Representatives, where, after heated debate on whether the new Restored Government of Virginia was legally competent under the Constitution, the bill passed on December 10, 1862, by a vote of 96 to 55. All that was left was for President Lincoln to sign the bill into law.

It should be noted at this point that the votes in the House approving the bill were not enough to overcome a presidential veto

Arthur Boreman, first governor of West Virginia. Library of Congress.

should Lincoln choose not to approve the bill. The bill sat on Lincoln's desk for over two weeks, raising concerns among the new leaders of the new state. Lincoln, it seems, was harboring private concerns over the advisability of creating a new state at the expense of Virginia, and over the bill's constitutionality. After all, if the legislature of the Old Dominion voted to withdraw from the Union, did not that legislature give up its authority (and protection) under the US Constitution? Lincoln said that Virginia could not have it both ways—both rejecting the Constitution of the United States by seceding, and then claiming its protection from dismemberment on the other.

On December 23, Lincoln put the question to the members of his cabinet. The cabinet split evenly on the issue, three supporting West Virginia statehood, three opposing. Attorney General Edward Bates, Secretary of the Navy Gideon Welles, and Postmaster General Montgomery Blair opposed admission, while Secretary of State William Seward, Secretary of the Treasury Salmon Chase, and Secretary of War Edwin Stanton favored admission. Among the concerns was the belief that allowing dismemberment of Virginia might make it difficult for that state to rejoin the Union.

While those opposing the bill believed the Restored Government was "technically" the representing government of Virginia during the war, they felt it was not the "constitutional" government and that it would cease to be following the war—it was merely the "interim" government. Those supporting statehood disagreed. For them, the Restored Government was the legitimate government of Virginia.

Lincoln, after listening to all of the arguments for and against, finally signed the bill on the eve of the new year. In doing so he wrote, "We can scarcely dispense with the aid of West Virginia in this struggle; much less can we afford to have her against us, in congress and in the field. Her brave and good men regard her admission into the Union as a matter of life and death. . . . I believe the admission of West Virginia into the Union is expedient."[11] "Expedient" is the key word.

Lincoln was above all else a pragmatic politician, and a competent lawyer. He saw the necessity and expediency of admitting the western counties of Virginia into the Union.

It seems clear that Lincoln favored statehood all along, and he polled his cabinet to test which arguments would prove most effective in accepting the requested admission. After all, the leaders of the Confederacy maintained from the very beginning that the US Constitution acknowledged secession. Was not western Virginia seceding from Virginia? By seceding it chose to remain in the Union and support the US Constitution, not reject it. How was this any different than Virginia's seceding from the Union? On signing the bill, Lincoln pointed out to its opponents, "It is said that the admission of West Virginia is secession, and tolerated only because it is our secession. Well, if we call it by that name, there is still difference enough between secession against the constitution, and secession in favor of the constitution."[12]

Lincoln issued a proclamation setting June 20, 1863, as the date West Virginia would join the Union as the thirty-fifth state. It was the first state to be admitted to the Union since the war had begun, and, ironically, was admitted as a slave state. While opponents of West Virginia statehood claimed the act was unconstitutional, the fact remains that it was a war measure brought about by secession. The fault resided with those Virginians who voted to leave the Union and, in doing so, no longer abided by the US Constitution. In one sense, West Virginia was the only land taken from the defeated foe as a result of the war. Few events during the war were as paradoxical or as convoluted as the birth of West Virginia. As with so many important issues decided during this turbulent period of history, might made right. One thing, however, is clear: the formation and admission of West Virginia as the thirty-fifth state to the Union was constitutional. Those who still decry West Virginia's formation need to read its history. Abraham Lincoln's newest child was legitimate.

Acknowledgments

I would like to thank my good friends who advised, edited, criticized, designed, and otherwise helped make this book (and my others) possible. A special thanks is due to Joseph Garrera, Executive Director of the Lehigh Valley Heritage Museum, for his many suggestions and editorial help. Joe is a true Lincoln scholar with keen insight into all things Lincoln. He has been a great help and good friend for many years. I also wish to thank Kieran McAuliffe, a longtime friend whose considerable skill in the graphic arts has proven invaluable to much of my work. I also thank Dr. James Cornelius for his many instructive suggestions concerning this book. I wish to thank Steven Wilson, Assistant Director and Curator of the Abraham Lincoln Library and Museum, for his generous support in providing access to the library and museum's collection. I also wish to acknowledge Lincoln scholar and artist Lloyd Ostendorf (now deceased), who over the years has been gracious in sharing his work with me and others. I also thank Jim Hoyt, who keeps my computer running so I do not have to. I thank Joseph Nichols for his overall editorial comments and suggestions regarding this book's content. I especially want to acknowledge the excellent support of the University Press of Kentucky's acquisitions editor Natalie O'Neal and Derik Shelor of Shelor and Son Publishing for their efforts in bringing this manuscript to publication. I also wish to recognize and thank my wife, Pat, who for sixty-six years has supported me in good times and bad with her love. And last but not least, to all the folks who buy, rent, or otherwise find my books, you do me honor. I thank you—and keep on reading.

Notes

1. The Shiftless Father Myth

1. "A Baby's Brain Development: The First Years Matter Most," onesky
.org.

2. Ibid.

3. Donald, *Lincoln*, 28.

4. Christopher Hitchens, "Lincoln's Emancipation," *The Atlantic*,
July–August 2009, 290.

5. Warren, *Lincoln's Parentage and Childhood*, 135.

6. Fehrenbacher and Fehrenbacher, eds., *Recollected Words of Abraham Lincoln*, 240–241.

7. Warren, *Lincoln's Parentage and Childhood*.

8. Barton, *The Lineage of Lincoln*; Barton, *The Paternity of Abraham Lincoln*.

9. *The Lincoln Kinsman* was published in fifty-two pamphlets between
1938 and 1942 by the Fort Wayne Lincoln Museum, sponsored by the Lincoln National Life Foundation, of which Louis Warren was the director.

10. Burlingame, *Abraham Lincoln: A Life*, 1:15.

11. Herndon and Weik, *Herndon's Life of Lincoln*, vii.

12. Louis A. Warren, "The Shiftless Father Myth," *Lincoln Kinsman*, no.
32 (February 1941).

13. Fehrenbacher and Fehrenbacher, *Recollected Words*, 395–396.

14. Quoted in Burlingame, *Abraham Lincoln: A Life*, 1:16.

15. Warren, *Lincoln's Parentage and Childhood*, 10–11.

16. Barton, *The Lineage of Lincoln*, 77–83.

17. Ibid., 69–70.

18. Governor Greenup Papers, Kentucky Department for Libraries and
Archives, Frankfort, Kentucky, Greenup/Military Appointments/August–
October 1805, folder 13, item GR3-38; Barton, *The Lineage of Lincoln*, 282.

19. Warren, *Lincoln's Parentage and Childhood*, 113.

20. Ibid., 47, 305; Barton, *The Lineage of Lincoln*, 289–292. Lincoln sold the farm eleven years later to Charles Melton for 100 pounds, less than the original price due to a faulty survey resulting in eighteen fewer acres.

21. Barton, *The Lineage of Lincoln*, 287.

22. Ibid., 292.

23. Ibid., 78–79.

24. Ibid., 289.

25. Warren, *Lincoln's Parentage and Childhood*, 117–118.

26. Louis A. Warren, "Abraham Lincoln's Father: A Chronological Table of References to Him in Authentic Records," *The Lincoln Kinsman*, no. 9 (March 1939).

27. Burlingame, *Abraham Lincoln: A Life*, 1:2–6.

28. Ibid., 1:6.

29. Ibid.

30. Judgments and Other Papers, Bundle 1808–1809, Hardin County Court, quoted in Warren, *Lincoln's Parentage and Childhood*, 333–334.

31. Wilson and Davis, eds., *Herndon's Informants*, 118.

32. While *Herndon's Informants* is the most complete compilation of material collected from those who knew Lincoln, it contains many reminiscences of a questionable nature recorded decades after many of the events occurred.

33. Louis A. Warren, "Dennis Friend Hanks," *The Lincoln Kinsman*, no. 45 (March 1942).

34. Suzanne W. Hallstrom, Nancy C. Royce, Stephan A. Whitlock, Richard G. Hileman, and Gerald M. Haslam, "Nancy Hanks Lincoln mtDNA Study: Unlocking the Secrets of Abraham Lincoln's Maternal Ancestry," geneticlincoln.com, 2015.

35. Wilson and Davis, eds., *Herndon's Informants*, 36.

36. Ibid., 176.

37. Ibid., 37.

38. Ibid., 37, 39.

39. Ibid., 107.

40. Ibid., 107–108.

41. Ibid., 37.

42. Warren, *Lincoln's Parentage and Childhood*, 142, 195, 206.

43. Burlingame, *Abraham Lincoln: A Life*, 1:42.

44. *Chicago Times-Herald*, August 25, 1895.

45. Blumenthal, *The Political Life of Abraham Lincoln*, 29.

46. Ibid., 22, 24.

47. McMurtry, *The Kentucky Lincolns on Mill Creek*, 9–11.

48. Ibid., 11–12.

49. Hallstrom et al., "Nancy Hanks Lincoln mtDNA Study."

50. Warren, *Lincoln's Parentage and Childhood*, 113.

51. Mary Lincoln had given birth to William Wallace "Willie" Lincoln two weeks earlier, following the death of young Edward Baker "Eddy" Lincoln eleven months before. It was an especially difficult time for Mary Lincoln, having lost one young son and given birth to another, which explains Lincoln's reluctance to leave her and travel to Charleston, Illinois.

52. Basler, ed. *The Collected Works of Abraham Lincoln*, 2:96–97.

53. Burlingame, *Abraham Lincoln: A Life*, 1:360.

54. Richard E. Hart, "Thomas Lincoln Reconsidered," *For the People* 18, no. 1 (spring 2016): 9–10.

55. Thomas "Tad" Lincoln was born on April 4, 1853, and died July 15, 1871, at the age of eighteen. His cause of death is unknown, but theories include tuberculosis, pneumonia, or congestive heart failure.

56. Zall, ed., *Abe Lincoln Laughing*, x.

2. A Case of Identity Theft

1. David Rankin Barbee quoted in Michael Burlingame, "New Light on the Bixby Letter," *Journal of the Abraham Lincoln Association* 16, no. 1 (winter 1995): 59.

2. Burlingame, "New Light on the Bixby Letter," 59–71.

3. Burlingame, *Abraham Lincoln: A Life*, 2:737.

4. Basler, ed., *The Collected Works of Abraham Lincoln*, 8:116–117.

5. Bullard, *Abraham Lincoln and the Widow Bixby*, 16.

6. Ibid., 17.

7. Burlingame, *Abraham Lincoln: A Life*, 2:737.

8. Bullard, *Abraham Lincoln and the Widow Bixby*, 54.

9. Ibid., 113.

10. Burlingame, "New Light on the Bixby Letter," 600.

11. Ibid., 59–71.

12. Joe Nickell, "Lincoln's Bixby Letter: A Study in Authenticity," *Lincoln Herald* 91, no. 4 (winter 1989): 135–140.

13. Ibid., 139.

14. Ibid.

15. Ibid.

16. The word "disenthrall" can be found only once in Lincoln's writings—his "Annual Message to Congress." See Basler, ed., *The Collected Works of Abraham Lincoln*, 5:518.

17. Burlingame, "New Light on the Bixby Letter," 65–66.

18. Nickell, "Lincoln's Bixby Letter," 139.

19. Abraham Lincoln message to Congress in Basler, ed., *The Collected Works of Abraham Lincoln*, 5:537.

20. Bullard, *Abraham Lincoln and the Widow Bixby*, 95–96.

21. http://en.wikipedia.org/wiki/Isaac_Markens.

22. Angle, ed., *A Portrait of Abraham Lincoln in Letters by His Oldest Son*, 38.

23. Steers, *Lincoln Legends*, 38.

24. Jack Grieve, Emily Carmody, Isobelle Clarke, Hannah Gideon, Annina Heini, Andrea Nini, and Emily Waibel, "Attributing the Bixby Letter Using N-Gram Tracing," *Digital Scholarship in the Humanities* 22 (May 2017): 251–270.

25. Michael Burlingame, "Abraham Lincoln and the Springfield Dispatches of Henry Villard, 1860–1861," talk delivered at the Abraham Lincoln Institute Symposium at Ford's Theatre, Washington, D.C., 16 March 2019.

26. Thomas Proisl, Stefan Evert, Fotis Jannidis, Christof Schoch, Leonard Konle, and Steffaen Pielstrom, "Delta vs. N-Gram Tracing: Evaluating the Robustness of Authorship Attribution Methods," *Proceedings of the Eleventh International Conference*, Miyazaki, Japan, 2018, 3309–3314.

27. Ibid., 3309.

28. Ibid., 3311.

29. Ibid., 3313.

3. Abe and Ann

1. Fehrenbacher and Fehrenbacher, eds., *Recollected Words of Abraham Lincoln*, 335–336. The Fehrenbachers rate these words a "D," a quotation about whose authenticity there is more than average doubt.

2. Paul H. Verduin, "Brief Outline of the Joseph Hanks Family," in Wilson and Davis, eds., *Herndon's Informants*, 779–783.

3. Herndon and Weik, *Herndon's Life of Lincoln*, 58. Don E. Fehren-

bacher and Virginia Fehrenbacher, in their book *Recollected Words of Abraham Lincoln*, write that while the incident may well have taken place as described, the recollected words of Lincoln appear to be "a fabrication." Fehrenbacher and Fehrenbacher, eds., *Recollected Words of Abraham Lincoln*, 238.

4. In 1828, Lincoln, along with Allen Gentry, had piloted a flatboat of goods down the Ohio and Mississippi Rivers to New Orleans for Allen's father, James Gentry. See Campanella, *Lincoln in New Orleans*.

5. Wilson and Davis, eds., *Herndon's Informants*, 456.

6. Quoted in Campanella, *Lincoln in New Orleans*, 147. This excellent book is the most thoroughly researched account of Lincoln's flatboat experiences.

7. Autobiography written for John L. Scripps, in Basler, ed., *The Collected Works of Abraham Lincoln*, 4:64.

8. William G. Greene interview in Wilson and Davis, eds., *Herndon's Informants*, 21.

9. Mentor Graham interview in Wilson and Davis, eds., *Herndon's Informants*, 242.

10. Robert L. Wilson in William G. Greene interview in Wilson and Davis, eds., *Herndon's Informants*, 201.

11. Abner Y. Ellis in William G. Greene interview in Wilson and Davis, eds., *Herndon's Informants*, 170.

12. Letter from N. W. Branson to William Herndon, August 3, 1865, in Wilson and Davis, eds., *Herndon's Informants*, 91.

13. John McNamar's real name was John McNeil. On leaving his home in Ohio, New York, McNeil opted to use an alias so no one could trace him in his new life. He was known by all in New Salem as John McNamar.

14. Thomas, *Lincoln's New Salem*, 81.

15. John Locke Scripps quoted in Wilson and Davis, eds., *Herndon's Informants*, xiv.

16. Wilson and Davis, eds., *Herndon's Informants*.

17. Herndon, *Lincoln and Ann Rutledge and the Pioneers of New Salem*, 3.

18. Turner and Turner, eds., *Mary Todd Lincoln*, 416.

19. See Wilson and Davis, eds., *Herndon's Informants*, 256, 266, 380–381, 381–387, 402–403, 408–409, 426–427, 497–498, 558.

20. David Rutledge was Ann's younger brother who died in 1842, seven years after Ann. Any statements from David concerning Ann are by definition hearsay.

21. Robert B. Rutledge interview in Wilson and Davis, eds., *Herndon's Informants*, 383.

22. Lewis Gannett, "'Overwhelming Evidence' of a Lincoln-Ann Rutledge Romance? Reexamining Rutledge Family Reminiscences," *Journal of the Abraham Lincoln Association*, 26, no. 1 (winter 2005): 31.

23. Ibid. 48.

24. Mentor Graham letter to Herndon, April 2, 1866, in Wilson and Davis, eds., *Herndon's Informants*, 243.

25. Robert B. Rutledge letter to Herndon, November 21, 1866, in Wilson and Davis, *Herndon's Informants*, 409.

26. Isaac Cogdal letter to Herndon, undated but in 1865 or 1866, in Wilson and Davis, eds., *Herndon's Informants*, 440.

27. C. A. Tripp, "The Strange Case of Isaac Cogdal," *Journal of the Abraham Lincoln Association* 23, no. 1 (winter 2002): 70–71.

28. Ibid., 73.

29. Ibid., 76.

30. Mentor Graham letter to Herndon, April 2, 1866, in Wilson and Davis, eds., *Herndon's Informants*, 243; Robert B. Rutledge letter to Herndon, November 21, 1866, in Wilson and Davis, eds., *Herndon's Informants*, 409.

31. One interesting example is the case of those who believe second- and thirdhand hearsay sources who claim that John Hay told them he was the author of the Bixby letter (see chapter 2).

32. John McNamar in a letter to G. U. Miles, 5 May 1866, in Wilson and Davis, eds., *Herndon's Informants*, 252–253.

33. John McNamar letter to Herndon, December 1, 1866, in Wilson and Davis, eds., *Herndon's Informants*, 493.

34. Thomas, *Lincoln's New Salem*, 66.

35. Abraham Lincoln letter to Mary S. Owens, May 7, 1837, in Basler, ed., *The Collected Works of Abraham Lincoln*, 1:78.

36. Ibid., 1:94.

37. Mary Owens Vineyard letter to Herndon, May 23, 1866, in Wilson and Davis, eds., *Herndon's Informants*, 254.

38. John Hill letter to Herndon, June 6, 1865, in Wilson and Davis, eds., *Herndon's Informants*, 25. The full text of this article also appears in Jay Monaghan, "New Light on the Lincoln-Rutledge Romance," *Abraham Lincoln Quarterly* 3, no. 3 (September 1944): 142–145.

39. Abraham Lincoln letter to John Hill, September 1860, in Basler, ed., *The Collected Works of Abraham Lincoln,* 4:104–108.

40. John Hill letter to Herndon, June 6, 1865, in Wilson and Davis, eds., *Herndon's Informants,* 23–25.

41. Basler, ed., *The Collected Works of Abraham Lincoln,* 4:104n1.

42. Parthena Hill letter to Herndon, March 1887, in Wilson and Davis, eds., *Herndon's Informants,* 409.

43. Monaghan, "New Light on the Lincoln-Rutledge Romance," 142.

44. Randall, *Lincoln the President,* 1:322–323.

45. Current, *The Lincoln Nobody Knows,* 41.

4. Proof from beyond the Grave

1. Weeks, *My Green Age,* 129.

2. Ibid., 251.

3. Edward Weeks quoted in Don E. Fehrenbacher, *The Minor Affair: An Adventure in Forgery and Detection,* The Second R. Gerald McMurty Lecture Delivered at Fort Wayne, Indiana (Fort Wayne, Indiana: Louis A. Warren Lincoln Library and Museum, 1979), 8.

4. Barton, *The Life of Abraham Lincoln;* Barton, *The Women Lincoln Loved.*

5. Quoted in Fehrenbacher, *The Minor Affair,* 13.

6. Tarbell, *The Life of Abraham Lincoln.*

7. Quoted in Fehrenbacher, *The Minor Affair,* 14.

8. Weeks, *My Green Age,* 255.

9. Sandburg, *Abraham Lincoln: The Prairie Years.*

10. Published separately as Herndon, *Lincoln and Ann Rutledge and the Pioneers of New Salem.*

11. Wilma Frances Minor, "Lincoln the Lover: I. The Setting—New Salem," *Atlantic Monthly,* December 1928, 838.

12. Ibid.

13. Wilma Frances Minor, "Lincoln the Lover: II. The Courtship," *Atlantic Monthly,* January 1929, 7.

14. Ibid., 8.

15. Wilma Frances Minor, "Lincoln the Lover: III. The Tragedy," *Atlantic Monthly,* February 1929, 216. It should be noted that Ann's mother was alive at the time.

16. Ibid., 42.

17. Ibid.

18. Ibid.

19. Thomas, *Lincoln's New Salem*, 82.

20. Minor, "Lincoln the Lover: III. The Tragedy," 42.

21. Baber, *A. Lincoln with Compass and Chain*, 6.

22. Fehrenbacher, *The Minor Affair*, 20.

23. Paul Angle, "The Minor Collection: A Criticism," *Atlantic Monthly*, April 1929, 522.

5. The Great White Father and the Dakota 38

Epigraph: Bennett, *Forced into Glory*, 165.

1. Kentucky did not become a state until 1792; until then it was the westernmost county of Virginia.

2. Abraham Lincoln letter to Jesse Fell, December 20, 1859, in Basler, ed., *The Collected Works of Abraham Lincoln*, 3:511.

3. Ibid., 3:512.

4. Sandburg, *Abraham Lincoln: The Prairie Years*, 1:155–156.

5. Niebuhr, *Lincoln's Bishop*, 90.

6. North Dakota and South Dakota were admitted to the Union on the same day, November 2, 1889, as the thirty-ninth and fortieth states, respectively.

7. Niebuhr, *Lincoln's Bishop*, 151.

8. Ibid., 46.

9. Ibid., 83.

10. Charles Bryant in 1864, two years after the war, collected dozens of personal accounts of brutal killings of white women and children. See Bryant, *A History of the Great Massacre by the Sioux Indians in Minnesota*.

11. Ibid., 315.

12. Ibid., 108.

13. Ibid., 339–340.

14. Niebuhr, *Lincoln's Bishop*, 98–99.

15. Porter was found guilty and dismissed from the army. In 1878, a special commission exonerated Porter and restored his commission as a colonel. See Eisenschiml, *The Celebrated Case of Fitz John Porter*.

16. Neely, *The Fate of Liberty*, 23, 129.

17. Whiting, *War Powers under the Constitution of the United States*.

18. Soldiers who violated the laws of war were tried by courts-martial.

19. Steers, ed., *The Trial*, 411.

20. Douglas O. Linder, "The Dakota Conflict Trials," http://law.umkc.edu/faculty/projects/ftrials/dakota.htm, 6.

21. Carol Chomsky, "The United States–Dakota War Trials: A Study in Military Injustice," *Stanford Law Review* 43, no. 1 (1990): 26.

22. Heard, *History of the Sioux War and Massacres of 1862 and 1863*, 44.

23. Niebuhr, *Lincoln's Bishop*, 145.

24. Abraham Lincoln letter to John Pope, November 10, 1862, in Basler, ed., *The Collected Works of Abraham Lincoln*, 5:493.

25. Quoted in Niebuhr, *Lincoln's Bishop*, 146.

26. Basler, ed., *The Collected Works of Abraham Lincoln*, 5:526.

27. Ibid.

28. Quoted in Nichols, *Lincoln and the Indians*, 117.

29. Basler, ed., *The Collected Works of Abraham Lincoln*, 5:551.

30. Subsequently, two more Dakota Indians were found guilty and hanged.

31. Chomsky, "The United States–Dakota War Trials," 14.

32. Basler, ed., *The Collected Works of Abraham Lincoln*, 5:551.

33. Chomsky, "The United States–Dakota War Trials," 29.

34. Bryant, *A History of the Great Massacre*, 1864; Nichols, *Lincoln and the Indians*, 1978; Niebuhr, *Lincoln's Bishop*, 2014.

35. Chomsky, "The United States–Dakota War Trials," 88.

36. Nichols, *Lincoln and the Indians*, 101–103.

37. Steers, ed., *The Trial*, 411.

38. Carol Chomsky, "The United States–Dakota War Trials," 226.

39. Quoted in Nichols, *Lincoln and the Indians*, 118.

40. Douglas O. Linder, "Dakota Conflict Trials: 1862," Encyclopedia.com (March 20, 2019), https://www.encyclopedia.com/law/law-magazines/dakota-conflict-trials-1862.

6. The Reluctant Emancipator

Epigraph: Bennett, *Forced into Glory*, 215.

1. John T. Hubbell, "Abraham Lincoln and the Recruitment of Black Soldiers," *Papers of the Abraham Lincoln Association* 2, no. 1 (1980): 6.

2. Stanley McChrystal, "Good Riddance," *Washington Post*, 21 November 2018.

3. U.S. Constitution, Amendment XIV, Section 1.

4. Bennett, *Forced into Glory*, 215.

5. Eugene R. Dattel, "Cotton and the Civil War," July 2008, http://www.mshistorynow.mdah.ms.gov/articles/291/cotton-and-the-civil-war; Eugene R. Dattel, "The South's Mighty Gamble on King Cotton," *American Heritage* 60, no. 2 (summer 2010): 2.

6. Hammond, *Selections from the Letters and Speeches of the Hon. James H. Hammond*, 124.

7. Dew, *Apostles of Disunion*, 51–52, 53.

8. Striner, *Lincoln and Race*, 1.

9. Basler, ed. *The Collected Works of Abraham Lincoln*, 3:16.

10. Don E. Fehrenbacher, "Only His Stepchildren: Lincoln and the Negro," *Civil War History* 20, no. 4 (December 1974): 303.

11. Whiting, *War Powers under the Constitution of the United States*.

12. Bennett, *Forced into Glory*, 7–8.

13. The Confiscation Act of 1862, passed on July 17, 1862, stated that any Confederate official who did not surrender within sixty days of the act's passage would have their slaves freed in criminal proceedings.

14. Bennett, *Forced into Glory*, 215.

15. Lincoln signed the contract the day before he released his Preliminary Emancipation Proclamation.

16. Liberia began as a settlement of the American Colonization Society (ACS), which believed blacks would have better chances for freedom and prosperity in Africa than in the United States. Liberia declared its independence in 1847, but it was not recognized until February 5, 1862, under Abraham Lincoln.

17. Basler, ed., *The Collected Works of Abraham Lincoln*, 2:337.

18. Ibid., 7:281.

19. Abraham Lincoln letter to Orville H. Browning, September 22, 1861, in Basler, ed., *The Collected Works of Abraham Lincoln*, 4:532.

20. Horace Greeley, "A Prayer for Twenty Millions," *New York Tribune*, August 20, 1862, 1.

21. Bennett, *Forced into Glory*, 215.

22. Ibid., 54.

23. Basler, ed., *The Collected Works of Abraham Lincoln*, 8:403.

24. Herndon and Weik, *Herndon's Life of Lincoln*, 353.

7. The Ailing Lincoln

Epigraph: Abraham Lincoln letter to Jesse Fell, December 20, 1859, in Basler, ed., *The Collected Works of Abraham Lincoln*, 3:512.

1. Wilson and Davis, eds., *Herndon's Informants*, 588.
2. Herndon and Weik, *Herndon's Life of Lincoln*, 471–472.
3. Wilson and Davis, eds., *Herndon's Informants*, 201–202.
4. Schwartz, "Abraham Lincoln and the Marfan Syndrome," 111–117.
5. For more on *forme fruste*, see https://en.wikipedia.org/wiki/Forme_fruste.
6. Schwartz, "Abraham Lincoln and the Marfan Syndrome," 112.
7. Wilson and Davis, eds., *Herndon's Informants*, 28.
8. Schwartz, "Abraham Lincoln and the Marfan Syndrome," 111.
9. Ibid., 116.
10. Ibid.
11. Ibid.
12. Details on Lincoln's glasses come from http://www.antiquespectacles.com/topics/lincoln/lincoln.htm.
13. Herndon and Weik, *Herndon's Life of Lincoln*, 70.
14. Ibid., 103.
15. Recent studies have shown that the survival age has dramatically increased due to better diagnoses of milder cases and cardiac surgery.
16. Wilson and Davis, eds., *Herndon's Informants*, 113.
17. Sotos, *The Physical Lincoln*.
18. https://www.nih.gov/about-nih/what-we-do/nih.../national-cancer-institute.
19. Sotos, *The Physical Lincoln*, 240.
20. Ibid., 125.
21. C. Gómez, I. Gavara, J. L. Ponce Marco, T. Belda Ibañez, A. Boscà Robledo, C. Sebastian Pastor, R. Navarro Milla, M. Caballero Soto, and M. Meseguer Anastasio, "The Optimal Age for Performing Surgery on Patients with MEN 2B Syndrome," *Oncology Letters* 2, no. 5 (September 2011): 929–930.
22. There also exist two life masks and the casts of Lincoln's two hands.
23. Norbert Hirschorn, Robert G. Feldman, and Ian A. Greaves, "Abraham Lincoln's Blue Pills," *Perspectives in Biology and Medicine* 44, no. 3 (summer 2001): 315.

24. Schroeder-Lein, *Lincoln and Medicine*, 15.

25. Wilson and Davis, eds., *Herndon's Informants*, 466.

26. Burlingame, *The Inner World of Abraham Lincoln*, 149.

27. Ibid.

28. Wilson and Davis, eds., *Herndon's Informants*, 443–444.

29. Burlingame, *The Inner World of Abraham Lincoln*, 148.

30. Wilson and Davis, eds., *Herndon's Informants*, 631–632.

31. Ibid., 205.

32. Ibid., 63, 193, 205, 236, 238, 243, 251, 266, 342, 374, 432, 466, 500, 626, 727.

33. www.nimh.nih.gov, Depression, 2014.

34. Burlingame, *The Inner World of Abraham Lincoln*, 92–113.

35. Henry C. Whitney quoted in ibid., 92.

36. Herndon and Weik, *Herndon's Life of Lincoln*, 265.

37. Burlingame, *The Inner World of Abraham Lincoln*, 154.

38. Joshua Speed interview in Wilson and Davis, eds., *Herndon's Informants*, 719. Also, Burlingame, *Abraham Lincoln: A Life*, 1:198–199.

39. Oldstone, *Viruses, Plagues, and History*, 65.

40. Steiner, *Disease in the Civil War*, 10.

41. Moseley, *Milk Sickness Caused by White Snakeroot*, 1.

42. It was originally classified under the genus *Eupatorium* but was reclassified by botanists under the genus *Ageratina*.

43. *Dorland's Illustrated Medical Dictionary*, 1635.

44. Wyngaarden and Smith, eds., *Textbook of Medicine*, 1059.

45. David Donald letter to Edward Steers Jr., October 16, 1996, author's collection.

8. Trading with the Enemy

Epigraph: Higham, *Murdering Mr. Lincoln*, jacket.

1. Higham, *Murdering Mr. Lincoln*, jacket; Guttridge and Neff, *Dark Union*.

2. Harris, *Lincoln's Last Months*, 175.

3. Dattel, "Cotton and the Civil War," http://www.mshistorynow.mdah.ms.gov/articles/291/cotton-and-the-civil-war.

4. Basler, ed., *The Collected Works of Abraham Lincoln*, 4:487–488.

5. Barbara Hahn and Bruce E. Baker, "Cotton," https://www.essentialcivilwarcurriculum.com/cotton.html.

6. Jim Powell, "Impact on the British Cotton Trade," https://ldhi.li
brary.cofc.edu/exhibits/show/liverpools-abercromby-square/britain-and-
us-civil-war/impact-cotton-trade.

7. Hammond, *Selections from the Letters and Speeches*, 124.

8. Dattel, "Cotton and the Civil War," http://www.mshistorynow
.mdah.ms.gov/articles/291/cotton-and-the-civil-war.

9. Ibid.

10. David G. Surdam, "Traders or Traitors: Northern Cotton Trading
during the Civil War," *Business and Economic History* 28, no. 2 (winter 1999):
303.

11. Ibid., 304.

12. Basler, ed., *The Collected Works of Abraham Lincoln*, 8:163–164.

13. Surdam, "Traders or Traitors," 302.

14. Harris, *Lincoln's Last Months*, 181.

15. Ibid., 176.

16. Ibid., 187.

17. Higham, *Murdering Mr. Lincoln*, 23–24; Guttridge and Neff, *Dark
Union*, 97–98.

18. Surdam, "Traders or Traitors," 304.

19. Harris, *Lincoln's Last Months*, 189.

20. Guttridge and Neff, *Dark Union*; Higham, *Murdering Mr. Lincoln*.

21. William C. Harris letter to Edward Steers Jr., 12 April 2004, author's
collection.

22. Higham, *Murdering Mr. Lincoln*; Guttridge and Neff, *Dark Union*.

23. Higham, *Murdering Mr. Lincoln*, xvii.

24. Harris, *Lincoln's Last Months*, 180.

9. West Virginia

Epigraph: Davis, *The Rise and Fall of the Confederate Government*, 2:257.

1. Basler, ed., *The Collected Works of Abraham Lincoln*, 6:28.

2. Davis, *The Rise and Fall of the Confederate Government*, 2:258.

3. The historical background leading up to the formation of West Virginia is covered in an article by Edward Steers Jr., "*Montani Semper Liberi*:
The Making of West Virginia," *North and South* 3, no. 2 (January 2000): 18–33.

4. Moore, *A Banner in the Hills*, 45–46.

5. Ibid., 63–64.

6. *Luther v. Borden*, 48 U.S. 17 Howard 1 (1849).

7. United States Constitution, Article Four, Section Four.

8. *Luther v. Borden*, 48 U.S. 17 Howard 1 (1849).

9. *Congressional Globe*, 37th Cong., 1st Sess., [and *Congressional Globe*, 37th Cong., 1st Sess., 6 and 109] (Washington: Blair and Rives, 1861).

10. Among the names considered were Kanawha, Western Virginia, and Vandalia.

11. Basler, ed., *The Collected Works of Abraham Lincoln*, 6:28.

12. Ibid.

Bibliography

Angle, Paul M., ed. *A Portrait of Abraham Lincoln in Letters by His Oldest Son.* Chicago: Chicago Historical Society, 1968.

Baber, Adin. *A. Lincoln with Compass and Chain.* Kansas, Ill.: Privately printed by the author, 1968.

Barton, William E. *The Life of Abraham Lincoln.* 2 vols. Indianapolis, Ind.: Bobbs-Merrill, 1925.

———. *The Lineage of Lincoln.* Indianapolis, Ind.: Bobbs-Merrill, 1929.

———. *The Paternity of Abraham Lincoln.* New York: Doran, 1920.

———. *The Women Lincoln Loved.* Indianapolis, Ind.: Bobbs-Merrill, 1927.

Basler, Roy P., ed. *The Collected Works of Abraham Lincoln.* 8 vols. New Brunswick, N.J.: Rutgers Univ. Press, 1953.

Bennett, Lerone. *Forced into Glory: Abraham Lincoln's White Dream.* Chicago: Johnson, 1999.

Blumenthal, Sidney. *The Political Life of Abraham Lincoln: A Self-Made Man, 1809–1849.* New York: Simon and Schuster, 2016.

Bryant, Charles. *A History of the Great Massacre by the Sioux Indians in Minnesota.* 1864; reprint, Cincinnati, Ohio: Rickey and Carroll, 2004.

Bullard, F. Lauristan. *Abraham Lincoln and the Widow Bixby.* New Brunswick, N.J.: Rutgers Univ. Press, 1946.

Burlingame, Michael. *Abraham Lincoln: A Life.* 2 vols. Baltimore, Md.: Johns Hopkins Univ. Press, 2008.

———. *The Inner World of Abraham Lincoln.* Urbana: Univ. of Illinois Press, 1994.

Campanella, Richard. *Lincoln in New Orleans: The 1828–1831 Flatboat Voyages and Their Place in History.* Lafayette: Univ. of Louisiana at Lafayette Press, 2010.

Chomsky, Carol. "The United States–Dakota War Trials: A Study in Military Injustice." *Stanford Law Review* 43, no. 1 (1990): 13–98.

Bibliography

Current, Richard Nelson. *The Lincoln Nobody Knows.* New York: Hill and Wang, 1958.

Davis, Jefferson. *The Rise and Fall of the Confederate Government.* 2 vols. 1881; reprint, New York: Da Capo, 1990.

Dew, Charles B. *Apostles of Disunion: Southern Secession Commissioners and the Causes of the Civil War.* Charlottesville: Univ. Press of Virginia, 2001.

Donald, David Herbert. *Lincoln.* New York: Simon and Shuster, 1995.

Dorland's Illustrated Medical Dictionary. Philadelphia, Pa.: Saunders, 1974.

Eisenschiml, Otto. *The Celebrated Case of Fitz John Porter: An American Dreyfus Affair.* Indianapolis, Ind.: Bobbs-Merrill, 1950.

Fehrenbacher, Don E., and Virginia Fehrenbacher, eds. *Recollected Words of Abraham Lincoln.* Stanford, Calif.: Stanford Univ. Press, 1996.

Governor Greenup Papers. Kentucky Department for Libraries and Archives, Frankfort, Kentucky. Greenup/Military Appointments/August–October 1805, folder 13, item GR3-38.

Guttridge, Leonard, and Ray A. Neff. *Dark Union: The Secret Web of Profiteers, Politicians, and Booth Conspirators That Led to Lincoln's Death.* Hoboken, N.J.: Wiley and Sons, 2003.

Hammond, James Henry. *Selections from the Letters and Speeches of the Hon. James H. Hammond.* New York: Trow, 1866.

Harris, William C. *Lincoln's Last Months.* Cambridge, Mass.: Belknap Press of Harvard Univ. Press, 2004.

Hart, Richard E. *The Collected Works of Thomas Lincoln, Carpenter and Cabinetmaker.* Springfield, Ill.: Pigeon Creek, 2019.

Heard, Isaac V. D. *History of the Sioux War and Massacres of 1862 and 1863.* New York: Harper, 1863.

Herndon, William H. *Lincoln and Ann Rutledge and the Pioneers of New Salem. A Lecture by William H. Herndon.* Herrin, Ill.: Trovillion Private Press, 1945.

Herndon, William H., and Jesse Weik. *Herndon's Life of Lincoln.* 3 vols. 1889; reprint, New York: Da Capo, 1983.

Higham, Charles. *Murdering Mr. Lincoln: A New Detection of the 19th Century's Most Famous Crime.* Beverly Hills, Calif.: New Millennium, 2004.

McMurtry, R. Gerald. *The Kentucky Lincolns on Mill Creek.* Harrogate, Tenn.: Lincoln Memorial University, 1939.

Moore, George F. *A Banner in the Hills: West Virginia's Statehood.* New York: Appleton-Century-Crofts, 1963.

Bibliography

Moseley, Edwin Lincoln. *Milk Sickness Caused by White Snakeroot.* Bowling Green, Ohio: Ohio Academy of Science, 1941.

Neely, Mark E. *The Fate of Liberty: Abraham Lincoln and Civil Liberties.* New York: Oxford Univ. Press, 1991.

Nichols, David A. *Lincoln and the Indians: Civil War Policy and Politics.* Columbia: Univ. of Missouri Press, 1978.

Niebuhr, Gustav. *Lincoln's Bishop: A President, a Priest, and the Fate of 300 Dakota Sioux Warriors.* New York: Harper One, 2014.

Oldstone, Michael. *Viruses, Plagues, and History.* New York: Oxford Univ. Press, 2010.

Randall, James G. *Lincoln the President.* 4 vols. 1946; reprint, New York: Da Capo, 1997.

Sandburg, Carl. *Abraham Lincoln: The Prairie Years.* 2 vols. New York: Harcourt Brace, 1926.

Schroeder-Lein, Glenna R. *Lincoln and Medicine.* Carbondale: Southern Illinois Univ. Press, 2012.

Schwartz, Harold. "Abraham Lincoln and the Marfan Syndrome." *Journal of the American Medical Association* 187, no. 7 (February 15, 1964): 473–479.

Sotos, John G. *The Physical Lincoln.* Mt. Vernon, Va.: Mt. Vernon Book Systems, 2008.

Steers, Edward, Jr. *Lincoln Legends.* Lexington: Univ. Press of Kentucky, 2007.

———, ed. *The Trial.* Lexington: Univ. Press of Kentucky, 2003.

Steiner, Paul E. *Disease in the Civil War: Natural Biological Warfare in 1861–1865.* Springfield, Ill.: Thomas, 1968.

Striner, Richard. *Lincoln and Race.* Carbondale: Southern Illinois Univ. Press, 2012.

Tarbell, Ida M. *The Life of Abraham Lincoln.* 4 vols. New York: Lincoln Historical Society, 1900.

Thomas, Benjamin P. *Lincoln's New Salem.* Springfield, Ill.: Abraham Lincoln Association, 1934.

Turner, Justin G., and Linda Levitt Turner, eds. *Mary Todd Lincoln: Her Life and Letters.* New York: Fromm International Publishing, 1987.

Warren, Louis A. *The Lincoln Kinsman* (published in fifty-two pamphlets). Fort Wayne, Ind.: Fort Wayne Lincoln Museum, Lincoln National Life Foundation, 1938–1942.

Bibliography

——. *Lincoln's Parentage and Childhood: A History of the Kentucky Lincolns Supported by Documentary Evidence.* New York: Century, 1926.

Weeks, Edward. *My Green Age.* Boston, Mass.: Little, Brown, 1973.

Whiting, William. *War Powers under the Constitution of the United States.* Boston, Mass.: J. L. Shorey, 1862.

Wilson, Douglas L., and Rodney O. Davis, eds. *Herndon's Informants: Letters, Interviews, and Statements about Abraham Lincoln.* Urbana: Univ. of Illinois Press, 1998.

Wyngaarden, James B., and Lloyd H. Smith Jr., eds. *Textbook of Medicine.* Philadelphia, Pa.: Saunders, 1982.

Zall, Paul M., ed. *Abe Lincoln Laughing.* Berkeley: Univ. of California Press, 1982.

About the Author

Edward Steers Jr. (University of Pennsylvania, A.B., Ph.D.), is the author of twenty-six books and the leading authority on the assassination of Abraham Lincoln. He has authored nine books on Lincoln's death, including *Blood on the Moon*, *The Lincoln Assassination Conspirators*, *His Name Is Still Mudd*, and *The Lincoln Assassination Encyclopedia*. He served as an advisor to the President's Lincoln Bicentennial Commission and as a member of the West Virginia Lincoln Bicentennial Commission. Ed has appeared on numerous television and radio shows, including PBS's *Morning Edition* with Bob Edwards, the Canadian Broadcasting System's *Phil Connors Show*, Public Broadcasting's *American Experience*, CSPAN's *Book Notes* with Brian Lamb, The History Channel's *Hard Cover History*, and Fox network's *Crossfire* with Robert Novak, and he was interviewed by Matt Lauer on NBC's *Today Show*. Among the honors he has received are the Robert Miller Award by the Company of Military Historians, the "Person of the Year" award from the Lincoln Group of the District of Columbia, the Lincoln Group of New York's "Achievement Award," and the "Lifetime Award of Achievement for Enduring Scholarship in the Field of Lincoln Research" by the Lehigh Valley Heritage Museum. In 2015 Dr. Steers received the prestigious "Richard Nelson Current" award from the Lincoln Forum for "contributions to the spirit of Abraham Lincoln in both word and deed."

Index

AB stands for Abraham Lincoln.
Page numbers in italics indicate illustrative material.

Index

Index

Index

Lincoln, Abraham (AB) *(cont.)*
148–149; poverty, 5, 6; in state militia, 87–89
Lincoln, Abraham (AB's grandfather), 7, 86–87, *88*, 148, 149
Lincoln, Bersheba (AB's grandmother), 7, 19
Lincoln, Eddy (AB's son), 21, 129
Lincoln, Hannaniah (AB's distant cousin), 7
Lincoln, John (AB's great-grandfather), 148, 149
Lincoln, Josiah (AB's uncle), 7, 86
Lincoln, Mary Todd (AB's wife), 20, 21, 54, 136–137
Lincoln, Mordecai (AB's ancestor), 140, 149
Lincoln, Mordecai (AB's uncle), 7, 86
Lincoln, Mordecai II (AB's ancestor), 148, 149
Lincoln, Nancy Hanks (AB's mother), *5*; AB on, 2–3; as bastard, 3, 15–16; death, 14, 21, 43, 64, 144, 146, 148; education of AB, 18; Elizabethtown home, *8*, 8, 9; positive scholarly view of, 2
Lincoln, Richard (AB's ancestor), 148
Lincoln, Robert Todd (AB's son), 36, *37*, 128, 129
Lincoln, Samuel (AB's ancestor), 127, 148, 149
Lincoln, Sarah (AB's sister), 9, 64, 146
Lincoln, Sarah Bush Johnston (AB's stepmother), 2, 16–17, *17*, 22, 43, 62
Lincoln, Thomas (AB's father), *4*; carpentry skills, 11–13, *12*, *13*; conflicting scholarly views on, 2, 3–6, 21; death and burial, 13, 19–21, *21*, *22*; health, 19–20, 128, 148; Illinois relocation, 15, 43–45; Indian confrontation, 86–87; in militia, 8; property owned by, 6–8, *8*, 9–10, 149; relationship with AB, 16–21; status in community, 8–9
Lincoln, Thomas (AB's son), 21, 129

Lincoln, Willie (AB's son), 21, 129
Lindsey, Vachel, *160*
linguistic analysis, 32–40, 60
Little Crow, *84*, 89, 92, 96, 107
Lower Sioux Agency, 92
Luther, Martin, 166
Luther v. Borden, 164–166

Marfan syndrome, 126–132
Markens, Isaac, 36
Marsh, Matthew, 63
Marshall, William, 98
McChrystal, Stanley, 109
McNamar, John, 49, 51, 54, 55, 56, 62–63
Mdewakanton band of Dakota, 91
melancholia and depression, 55, 62, 63–64, 67–68, 78, 138–140
Mexican lands, 113
military tribunals, 96–102, 105–106
milk sickness, 14, 43, 144–147
Minnesota frontier, 89–90, *90. See also* Dakota Sioux
Minor, Wilma Frances: articles on Lincoln–Rutledge romance, 76–79; as fraud, 79–82; manuscript materials on Lincoln–Rutledge romance, 71–76, *72*
Monaghan, Jay, 69
Morley, John, 25, 30
multiple endocrine neoplasia 2B (MEN 2b), 132–134

Native Americans. *See* Dakota Sioux; Indians
naval blockades, 152, 153, 154
Neff, Ray, 157
Nevins, Allan, 76
New Salem, Illinois, establishment and growth, 48–50
N-gram analysis, 37–40
Nickell, Joe, 32–33
Nicolay, John George, 62

Office of Indian Affairs, 90–91, 100

Index

Index

smallpox, 142–143
snakeroot plant, 144, *145*
Sotos, John G., 132–134
Sparrow, Elizabeth and Thomas, 14, 146
Sparrow, Henry and Lucy Hanks, 15–16
Speed, Joshua, 125, 141–142
Stanton, Edwin M., 89, 154, *155*, 170
Striner, Richard, 114
Stuart, John T., 138
suffrage, 106, 122, 123
Swett, Eliza, 93
Swett, Leonard, 156, 157
syphilis, 140–142

Taney, Roger Brooke, 166
Tarbell, Ida Minerva, *74*, 74–75
text analysis, 32–40, 60
Thirteenth Amendment, 117–118, 122
Tiokasin Ghosthorse, 102
Tobin, Michael, 29
Todd, Robert, 21
Torrey, Fred Martin, *160*
trade policy, wartime: as controversial, 151, 154–158; naval blockades, 152, 153, 154; and Southern cotton economy, 111, 152–153; stipulations, 152, 153–154
Tripp, Charles A., 59–60
typhoid fever, 143–144

US Constitution: formation of states, 159–160, 168; republican government protected by, 166; slavery pro-tected by, 114–115; Thirteenth Amendment, 117–118, 122; three-fifths provision, 162; war powers of the president, 115–117
US Treasury Department, 152, 153, 156

vaccinations, 143
Variola (smallpox), 142–143
Virginia, *161; Luther v. Borden* precedent, 164–166; representation of western counties, 161–162; Restored Government of, 164, 166–168, 170; secession from Union, 160–161, 162–163; slavery in, 159, 162; West Virginia statehood approval, 159, 168–171; Wheeling Convention, 163–164
voting rights, 106, 122, 123

Wahpekute band of Dakota, 91
Waltz, Caroline, 93
war, laws of, 97–98, 104–105. *See also* Civil War; Dakota Sioux
Warren, Louis A., 3, 4–6, 11, 13
Weeks, Edward A., 71, 72–73
Welles, Gideon, 169
West Virginia, statehood approval, 159, 168–171. *See also* Virginia
Wheeling Convention (1861), 163–164
Whipple, Benjamin, *99*, 99–100
Whitney, Henry C., 137, 139–140
Willey, Thomas Waitman, 166, *167*, 168
Wilson, Douglas L., xii, 14, 52, 55
Wilson, Robert, 126, 138

Books by the Author

The Escape and Capture of John Wilkes Booth: A Guide
The Quotable Lincoln
His Name Is Still Mudd
Blood on the Moon
The Trial
Don't You Know There's a War On?
Hoax
Essays in History
Forgotten History
I'll Be Seeing You. A Novel
Der Tagebuch. A Novel
Port Hudson to Cedar Creek
The Lincoln Assassination Encyclopedia
The Lincoln Assassination Conspirators (with Harold Holzer)
Lincoln Legends
Caesar Must Bleed. A Novel
The Lincoln Assassination: The Evidence (with William C. Edwards)
Lincoln Slept Here: Lincoln Family Sites in America, 3 vols.